Travellers' Tu

David Ellis is Director
co-author of a number of language books.

Roderick Conway Morris studied Turkish at the School
of Oriental and African Studies in London, and is the author
of **Jem: Memoirs of an Ottoman Secret Agent**.

Other phrase books in the series

Travellers' **Dutch**
Travellers' **French**
Travellers' **German**
Travellers' **Greek**
Travellers' **Italian**
Travellers' **Japanese**
Travellers' **Portuguese**
Travellers' **Scandinavian**
Travellers' **Serbo-Croat**
Travellers' **Spanish**
Travellers' **Multilingual Phrase Book**

Travellers' **Turkish**

D. L. Ellis

Roderick Conway Morris

Pan Books London, Sydney and Auckland

Acknowledgements

Roderick Conway Morris would like to thank Professor
Süheyla Artemel of Boğaziçi University, Istanbul, for her
generous help and advice, and Dr Antony Greenwood and
the American Research Institute in Turkey for their
assistance and hospitality.

The publishers are also grateful to the Turkish Tourist and
Information Office in London for their help in the
preparation of this book.

First published 1989 by Pan Books Ltd,
Cavaye Place, London SW10 9PG
9 8 7 6 5 4 3 2 1
© D. L. Ellis and Roderick Conway Morris 1989
ISBN 0 330 30759 2

Phototypeset by Input Typesetting Ltd, London
Printed and bound in Great Britain by
Richard Clay Ltd, Bungay, Suffolk

Contents

Using the phrase book

- This phrase book is designed to help you get by in Turkey, to get what you want or need. It concentrates on the simplest but most effective way you can express these needs in an unfamiliar language.
- The **Contents** on p. 5 give you a good idea of which section to consult for the phrase you need.
- The **Index** on p. 142 gives you more detailed information about where to look for your phrase.
- When you have found the right page you will be given:
  either – the exact phrase
  or   – help in making up a suitable sentence
  and   – help in getting the pronunciation right.
- The English sentences in **bold type** will be useful for you in a variety of different situations, so they are worth learning by heart. (See also **Do it yourself**, p. 135.)
- Wherever possible you will find help in understanding what Turkish people say to you in reply to your questions.
- If you want to practise the basic nuts and bolts of the language further, look at the **Do it yourself** section starting on p. 135.
- Note especially these three sections:
  Everyday expressions, p. 10
  Shop talk, p. 50
  Public notices, p. 114.
  You are sure to want to refer to them most frequently.
- Once abroad, remember to make good use of the local tourist offices (see p. 22).

UK address:
The Turkish Tourist and Information Office
Egyptian House
170 Piccadilly
London W1V 9DD
Tel: 01-734 8681

A note on the pronunciation system

Turkish is not a difficult language for English speakers to pronounce, and the Turkish alphabet, although containing a few unfamiliar variations of letters, is almost identical to our own. So to make things easier and to help make the phrase book instantly usable without any preparation, below each sentence the words are written out in a simplified form. This system is not phonetical, but if you follow it what you say should be readily comprehensible to Turkish speakers. One thing to remember is to lay the stress on the syllables in italics, e.g. **iyi akşamlar** (ee-y*ee* ahk-shahm-l*ahr*): 'good evening/night'.

In fact the stress on words in Turkish tends to be more even than in English, with the emphasis usually falling on the last syllable of the word (although with place names it often falls on the first or second syllable). However, even if your pronunciation is not quite right you will generally find that you are understood, since most Turks are good and willing listeners and are genuinely pleased when foreigners take the trouble to try to speak Turkish.

Letter	Pronunciation	Letter	Pronunciation
A a	**a** as in father	L l	**l** as in long
Â â	**aa** as in baa	M m	**m** as in mother
B b	**b** as in but	N n	**n** as in no
C c	**j** as in judge	O o	**o** as in opera
Ç ç	**ch** as in chat	Ö ö	like **ea** in early
D d	**d** as in dot		
E e	**e** as in bed	P p	**p** as in pot
F f	**f** as in four	R r	**r** as in red
G g	**g** as in good	S s	**s** as in some
Ğ ğ	not pronounced, but makes the letter before slightly longer	Ş ş	**sh** as in shop
		T t	**t** as in tell
		U u	**u** as in put
H h	**h** as in have	Ü ü	as the Scots say the **u** in put
İ i	**i** as in sit		
I ı	**i** as in Cyril	V v	**v** as in very
J j	like **s** in pleasure	Y y	**y** as in yet
		Z z	**z** as in zero
K k	**k** as in kite		

Kolay gelsin! Roderick Conway Morris, 1989

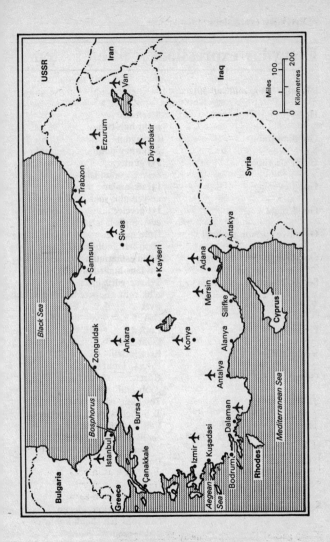

Everyday expressions

[*See also 'Shop talk', p. 50*]

Hello	**Merhaba** mehr-hah-bah
Good morning	**Günaydın** gooh-nay-duhn
Good afternoon	**İyi günler** ee-yee goohn-lehr
Good evening	**İyi akşamlar** ee-yee ahk-shahm-lahr
Good night	**İyi geceler** ee-yee gheh-jeh-lehr
Goodbye [*person staying*]	**Güle güle** gooh-leh gooh-leh
Goodbye [*person leaving*]	**Allahaısmarladık** ahl-lahs-mahr-lah-duhk
See you later	**Tekrar görüşürüz** tehk-rahr gher-rooh-shooh-roohz
Yes	**Evet** eh-vet
Please	**Lütfen** looht-fehn
Yes, please	**Evet lütfen** eh-vet, looht-fehn
Great!	**Güzel!** gooh-zehl
Thank you	**Teşekkür ederim** Teh-shehk-koohr eh-deh-reem
Thank you very much	**Çok teşekkür ederim** chohk teh-shehk-koohr eh-deh-reem
That's right	**Doğru** doh-roo
No	**Hayır** hah-yuhr
No, thank you	**Hayır, teşekkür ederim** hah-yuhr teh-shehk-koohr eh-deh-reem

I disagree	**Öyle değil**
	er-*leh* deh-*eel*
Excuse me ⌉	**Afferdersiniz**
Sorry ⌋	ahf-feh-dehr-see-*neez*
Don't mention it ⌉	**Bir şey değil**
That's OK ⌋	beer shehy dee-*eel*
That's good ⌉	**Tamam**
I like it ⌋	tah-m*a*hm
That's no good ⌉	**Tamam değil**
I don't like it ⌋	tah-m*a*hm dee-*eel*
I know	**Biliyorum**
	bee-*lee*-yoh-room
I don't know	**Bilmiyorum**
	b*eel*-mee-yoh-room
It doesn't matter	**Zararı yok**
	zah-rah-r*u*h yohk
Where's the toilet, please?	**Tuvalet nerede, lütfen?**
	too-wah-l*eh*t neh-reh-d*e*h *loo*ht-fehn
How much is that? [*point*]	**Bu ne kadar?**
	boo neh kah-d*a*hr
Is the service included?	**Servis dahil mi?**
	sehr-v*ee*s dah-h*ee*l mee
Do you speak English?	**İngilizce biliyor musunuz?**
	Een-ghee-l*ee*z-jeh bee-*lee*-yohr moo-soo-n*oo*z
I'm sorry . . .	**Özür dilerim . . .**
	er-z*oo*hr dee-leh-r*ee*m
I don't speak Turkish	**Türkçe bilmiyorum**
	t*oo*hrk-cheh b*ee*l-mee-yoh-room
I only speak a little Turkish	**Pek az Türkçe biliyorum**
	pehk ahz t*oo*hrk-cheh bee-*lee*-yoh-room
I don't understand	**Anlamıyorum**
	ahn-lah-muh-yoh-room
Please can you . . .	**Lütfen . . .**
	*loo*ht-fehn
repeat that	**tekrarlayınız**
	tehk-rahr-lah-yuh-n*uh*z
speak more slowly	**daha yavaş konuşunuz**
	dah-h*a*h yah-v*a*hsh koh-noo-shoo-n*oo*z

write it down	**yazınız** yah-zuh-n*uh*z
What is this called in Turkish? [*point*]	**Türkçe bunun adı ne?** t*oo*hrk-cheh boo-n*oo*n ah-d*uh* neh

Crossing the border

ESSENTIAL INFORMATION

- Don't waste time before you leave rehearsing what you're going to say to the border officials – the chances are that you won't have to say anything at all, especially if you travel by air.
- It is more useful to check that you have your documents handy for the journey: passport, tickets, money, travellers' cheques, insurance documents, driving licence and car registration documents.
- Look our for these signs:
  SINIR (border)
  DUR (stop)
  PASAPORT KONTROLU (passport control)
  GÜMRÜK (customs)
  KAMBİYO (exchange)
  VARIŞ (arrival)
  ÇIKIŞ (departure)
  [*For further signs and notices, see p. 114*]
- You may be asked routine questions by the customs officials [*see below*]. If you have to give personal details, see 'Meeting people', p. 13. The other important answer to know is 'Nothing': **Hiç** (heech).

ROUTINE QUESTIONS

Passport?	**Pasaport?** pah-sah-p*oh*rt
Insurance?	**Sigorta?** see-g*oh*r-tah

Driving licence?	**Şoför ehliyeti**
	shoh-f*er* eh-lee-yeh-t*ee*
Green card	**Yeşil kart**
	yeh-sh*ee*l kahrt
Ticket, please	**Bilet, lütfen**
	bee-l*eh*t l*oo*ht-fehn
Have you anything to declare?	**Deklare edecek bir şeyiniz var mı?**
	deh-klah-r*eh* eh-deh-jehk beer
	sheh-yee-n*ee*z vahr muh
Where are you going?	**Nereye gidiyorsunuz?**
	neh-reh-y*eh* ghee-d*ee*-yohr-soo-
	nooz
How long are you staying?	**Ne kadar kalacaksınız?**
	neh kah-d*a*hr kah-lah-jahk-suh-
	n*u*hz
Where have you come from?	**Nereden geldiniz?**
	neh-reh-d*eh*n ghehl-dee-n*ee*z

You may also have to fill in forms which ask for:

surname	**soyadı**
first name	**adı**
date of birth	**doğum tarihi**
address	**adres**
nationality	**uyruk**
profession	**meslek**
passport number	**pasaport numarası**
issued at	**verildiği yer**
place of birth	**doğum yeri**
signature	**imza**

Meeting people

[*See also 'Everyday expressions', p. 10*]

Breaking the ice

Hello	**Merhaba**
	m*e*hr-hah-bah

Good day	**İyi günler** ee-y*ee* goohn-lehr
How are you?	**Nasılsınız?** nah-suhl-suh-n*uh*z
I am well	**İyiyim** ee-yee-*yee*m
And you?	**Ya siz?** yah seez
Pleased to meet you	**Memnun oldum** mehm-n*oon* ohl-d*oo*m
I am here . . .	**Buradayım . . .** boo-rah-dah-y*uh*m
on holiday	**tatil için** tah-t*ee*l ee-cheen
on business	**iş için** eesh ee-cheen
Would you like . . .	**. . . ister misiniz?** ees-t*eh*r mee-see-n*ee*z
a drink?	**Bir içki** beer eech-k*ee*
a cigarette?	**Bir sigara** beer see-g*ah*-rah
a cigar?	**Bir puro** beer p*oo*-roh

Name

What's your name?	**Adınız ne?** ah-duh-n*uh*z neh
My name is . . .	**Adım . . .** ah-d*uh*m

Family

Are you married?	**Evli misiniz?** ehv-*lee* mee-see-n*ee*z
I am married	**Evliyim** ehv-lee-*yee*m
I am single	**Bekârım** beh-kyah-r*uh*m
This is . . .	**Bu . . .** boo

my wife	**eşim**
	eh-sh*eem*
my husband	**eşim**
	eh-sh*eem*
my son	**oğlum**
	oh-l*oom*
my daughter	**kızım**
	kuh-z*uh*m
my friend	**arkadaşım**
	ahr-kah-dah-sh*uh*m
my colleague	**meslektaşım**
	mehs-lehk-tah-sh*uh*m
Do you have any children?	**Çocuğunuz var mı?**
	choh-joo-oo-n*ooz* vahr muh
I have . . .	**. . . var**
	vahr
one daughter	**Bir kızım**
	beer kuh-z*uh*m
one son	**Bir oğlum**
	beer oh-l*oom*
two daughters	**İki kızım**
	ee-k*ee* kuh-z*uh*m
three sons	**Üç oğlum . . .**
	oohch oh-l*oom*
No, I haven't any children	**Hayır, çocuğum yok**
	h*ah*-yuhr choh-joo-*oo*m yohk

Where you live

Are you Turkish?	**Türk müsünüz?**
	toohrk mooh-sooh-n*oo*hz
I am English	**İngilizim**
	een-ghee-leez-*ee*m
I am American	**Amerikalıyım**
	ah-meh-ree-kah-luh-y*uh*m

[*For other nationalities, see p. 128*]

Where are you from?

I am . . .	**Ben . . .**
	behn
from London	**Londra'dan**
	lohn-drah-dahn

from England	**İngiltere'den** een-gheel-teh-reh-dehn
from New York	**New York'tan** New York-tahn
from America	**Amerika'dan** ah-mehr-ree-kah-dahn
from the north	**kuzeyden** koo-zehy-dehn
from the south	**güneyden** gooh-nehy-dehn
from the east	**doğudan** doh-oo-dahn
from the west	**batıdan** bah-tuh-dahn
from the centre	**ortadan** ohr-tah-dahn

[*For other countries, see p. 127*]

For the businessman and woman

I'm from . . . (firm's name)	**Ben . . . (firm's name) 'denim** ben (. . .)-deh-neem
I have an appointment with . . .	**(person's name) . . . ile randevum var** (. . .) ee-leh rahn-deh-voom vahr
May I speak to . . .?	**(person's name) . . . ile görüşebilir miyim?** (. . .) ee-leh ger-oohsh-eh-bee-leer mee-yeem
This is my card	**İşte kartım** eesh-teh kahr-tuhm
I'm sorry I'm late	**Geç kaldığım için özür dilerim** ghech kahl-duh-uhm ee-cheen er-zoohr dee-leh-reem
Can I fix another appointment?	**Başka bir randevu alabilir miyim?** bahsh-kah beer rahn-deh-voo ah-lah-bee-leer mee-yeem
I'm staying at the (Hilton) hotel	**(Hilton) otelinde kalıyorum** (heel-tohn) oh-teh-leen-deh kah-luh-yoh-room
I'm staying in (Meşrutiyet) Avenue	**(Meşrutiyet) Caddesinde kalıyorum** (mehsh-roo-tee-yeht) jahd-deh-seen-deh kah-luh-yoh-room

Asking the way

ESSENTIAL INFORMATION

• Keep a look-out for all these place names as you will find them on shops, maps and notices.

WHAT TO SAY

Excuse me, please

Affedersiniz, efendim
ahf-feh-dehr-see-n*eez* eh-f*eh*n-deem

How do I get . . .

. . . nasıl gidebilirim?
nah-s*u*hl ghee-deh-bee-*lee*-reem

to Ankara?

Ankara'ya
*a*hn-kah-rah-yah

to Istanbul?

İstanbul'a
ee-st*a*hn-boo-lah

to (Cumhuriyet) Avenue?

(Cumhuriyet) Caddesine
(juhm-h*oo*-ree-yeht) jahd-deh-see-neh

to the (Pera Palas) hotel?

(Pera Palas) oteline
(p*eh*-rah pah-l*a*hs) oh-teh-lee-neh

to the airport?

Hava meydanına
hah-v*a*h mey-dah-nuh-n*a*h

to the beach?

Plaja
plah-zh*a*h

to the bus station?

Otobüs durağına
oh-toh-b*oo*hs doo-rah-uh-n*a*h

to the historic site?

Tarihi yere
tah-ree-h*ee* yeh-r*e*h

to the police station?

Karakola
kah-rah-koh-l*a*h

to the port?

Limana
lee-mah-n*a*h

to the (ferry) landing?

İskeleye
ees-keh-leh-yeh

to the post office?

Postaneye
poh-stah-neh-yeh

to the railway station?

İstasyona
ee-stahs-yoh-n*a*h

to the sports stadium?	**Stadyuma**
	stahd-yoo-m*ah*
to the tourist information office?	**Danışma bürosuna**
	dah-nuhsh-m*ah* booh-roh-soo-n*ah*
to the town centre?	**Şehir merkezine**
	sheh-h*ee*r mehr-keh-zee-n*eh*
to the town hall?	**Belediye dairesine**
	beh-leh-dee-y*eh* dy-reh-see-n*eh*
Excuse me	**Affedersiniz**
	ahf-feh-dehr-see-n*eez*
Is there . . . nearby?	**Civarda . . . var mı?**
	jee-vahr-d*ah* . . . vahr muh
an art gallery	**bir sanat galerisi**
	beer sah-n*ah*t gah-leh-ree-s*ee*
a baker's	**bir fırıncı**
	beer fuh-ruhn-j*uh*
a bank	**bir banka**
	beer b*ah*n-kah
a bar	**bir bar**
	beer bahr
a bus stop	**bir otobüs durağı**
	beer oh-toh-boohs doo-rah-*uh*
a butcher's	**bir kasap**
	beer kah-s*ah*p
a café	**bir kafe**
	beer kah-f*eh*
a cake shop	**bir pastane**
	beer pah-st*ah*-neh
a campsite	**bir kamp yeri**
	beer kahmp yeh-r*ee*
a car park	**bir park**
	beer pahrk
a change bureau	**bir kambiyo**
	beer k*ah*m-bee-yoh
a chemist's	**bir eczane**
	beer ehj-z*ah*-neh
a church	**bir kilise**
	beer kee-l*ee*-seh
a cinema	**bir sinema**
	beer see-neh-m*ah*
a concert hall	**bir konser salonu**
	beer kohn-s*eh*r sah-loh-n*oo*

a delicatessen	**bir şarküteri**
	beer shah-kooh-teh-r*ee*
a dentist	**bir dişçi**
	beer deesh-ch*ee*
a department store	**bir büyuk mağaza**
	bir booh-y*oo*hk mah-ah-z*a*h
a disco	**bir diskotek**
	beer dees-koh-t*e*hk
a doctor	**bir doktor**
	beer dohk-t*o*hr
a dry cleaner's	**bir kuru temizleyici**
	beer koo-roo teh-meez-leh-yee-j*ee*
a fishmonger's	**bir balıkçı**
	beer bah-luhk-ch*u*h
a garage (for repairs)	**bir tamirhane**
	beer tah-meer-hah-n*e*h
a hairdresser's	**bir kuaför**
	beer kwah-f*e*r
a greengrocer's	**bir manav**
	beer mah-n*a*hv
a grocer's	**bir bakkal**
	beer bahk-k*a*hl
a hardware shop	**bir hırdavatçı**
	beer huhr-dah-vaht-ch*u*h
a hospital	**bir hastane**
	beer hah-st*a*h-neh
a hotel	**bir otel**
	beer *o*h-tehl
a laundry	**bir çamaşırhane**
	beer chah-mah-sh*u*hr-hah-neh
a mosque	**bir cami**
	beer jah-m*ee*
a museum	**bir müze**
	beer mooh-z*e*h
a newsagent's	**bir gazeteci**
	beer gah-zeh-teh-j*ee*
a nightclub	**bir gece kulübü**
	beer gheh-jeh koo-looh-b*oo*h
a park	**bir park**
	beer pahrk
a petrol station	**bir benzin deposu**
	beer behn-z*ee*n deh-poh-s*oo*

Is there . . . nearby?	**Civarda . . . var mi?**
	jee-vahr-d*ah* . . . vahr muh
a postbox	**bir posta kutusu**
	beer poh-stah koo-too-s*oo*
a restaurant	**bir lokanta**
	beer loh-k*ah*n-tah
a sports ground	**bir spor alanı**
	beer spohr ah-lah-n*uh*
a supermarket	**bir süpermarket**
	beer sooh-pehr-mahr-keht
a sweet shop	**bir şekerci**
	beer sheh-kehr-j*ee*
a swimming pool	**bir yüzme havuzu**
	beer yoohz-m*eh* hah-voo-z*oo*
a synagogue	**bir sinagog**
	beer see-nah-g*oh*g
a taxi stand	**bir taksi durağı**
	beer tahk-s*ee* doo-rah-*uh*
a telephone	**bir telefon**
	beer teh-leh-f*oh*n
a theatre	**bir tiyatro**
	beer tee-y*ah*-troh
a tobacconist's	**bir tütüncü**
	beer tooh-toohn-j*oo*
a toilet	**bir tuvalet**
	beer too-wah-l*e*t
a travel agent	**bir turizm acentası**
	beer too-r*ee*zm ah-jehn-tah-s*uh*
a zoo	**bir hayvanat bahçesi**
	beer hy-vah-n*ah*t bah-cheh-s*ee*

DIRECTIONS

- Asking where a place is, or if a place is nearby, is one thing; making sense of the answer is another.
- Here are some of the most important key directions and replies.

Left	**Sol**
	sohl
Right	**Sağ**
	sah

Straight on	**Düz**
	doohz
There	**Oraya/Orada**
	oh-rah-yah/oh-rah-dah
First (left/right)	**(Soldan/Sağdan) birinci**
	(sohl-dahn/sah-dahn) bee-reen-jee
Second (left/right)	**(Soldan/Sağdan) ikinci**
	(sohl-dahn/sah-dahn) ee-keen-jee
At the crossroads	**Kavşakta**
	kahv-shahk-tah
At the roundabout	**Dönel kavşakta**
	der-nehl kahv-shahk-tah
At the traffic lights	**Trafik lambasında**
	trah-feek lahm-bah-suhn-dah
It's near/far	**Yakın/uzak**
	yah-kuhn/oo-zahk
One kilometre	**Bir kilometre**
	beer kee-loh-meh-treh
Two kilometres	**İki kilometre**
	ee-kee kee-loh-meh-treh
Five minutes . . .	**Beş dakika**
	behsh dah-kee-kah
on foot	**yaya**
	yah-yah
by car	**araba ile**
	ah-rah-bah ee-leh
Take . . .	**. . . bininiz**
	bee-nee-neez
the bus	**Otobüse**
	oh-toh-booh-seh
the ferryboat	**Vapura**
	vah-poo-rah
the train	**Trene**
	treh-neh
the **dolmuş**	**Dolmuşa**
	dohl-moo-shah

[For public transport, see p. 105]

The tourist information office

ESSENTIAL INFORMATION

- All the main towns in Turkey, and many of the smaller ones, have tourist information offices. There are also information desks at airports and border crossings. There will usually be someone there who speaks English.
- Look out for this symbol:

  i

  and the following sign:
  DANIŞMA BÜROSU (information office)
- These offices can give you free information in the form of printed leaflets, fold-outs, brochures, maps, lists and plans.
- For finding a tourist office, see p. 17.

WHAT TO SAY

Please, have you got . . .	**Lütfen, . . . var mı?** looht-fehn . . . vahr muh
a plan of the town?	**bir şehir planı** beer sheh-heer plah-nuh
a list of hotels?	**bir otel listesi** beer oh-tehl lees-teh-see
a list of campsites?	**bir kamp listesi** beer kahmp lees-teh-see
a list of restaurants?	**bir lokanta listesi** beer loh-kahn-tah lees-teh-see
a list of events?	**bir önemli olaylar listesi** beer er-nehm-lee oh-ly-lahr lees-teh-see
a leaflet on the town?	**şehir hakkında bir broşür** sheh-heer hahk-kuhn-dah beer broh-shoohr
a leaflet on the region?	**bölge hakkında bir broşür** berl-gheh hahk-kuhn-dah beer broh-shoohr
a railway timetable?	**bir tren tarifesi** beer trehn tah-ree-feh-see

a bus timetable?	**bir otobüs tarifesi**
	beer oh-toh-*boohs* tah-ree-feh-*see*
In English, please	**İngilizçe, lütfen**
	een-ghee-*leez*-cheh *looht*-fehn
Can you recommend . . .	**. . . tavsiye edebilir misiniz?**
	tahv-see-*yeh* eh-deh-bee-*leer* mee-see-*neez*
a (cheap) hotel?	**(Ucuz) Bir otel**
	(oo-*jooz*) beer oh-t*ehl*
a (cheap) restaurant?	**(Ucuz) Bir lokanta**
	(oo-*jooz*) beer loh-k*ahn*-tah
Can you book a (room/table) for me?	**Bir (oda/masa) rezervasyonu yapabilir misiniz?**
	beer (oh-d*ah*/mah-s*ah*) reh-zehr-vahs-yoh-n*ooh* yah-pah-bee-*leer* mee-see-n*eez*

LIKELY ANSWERS

You need to understand when the answer is 'No'. You should be able to tell by the assistant's facial expression, tone of voice and gesture; but there are some language clues, such as:

No	**Hayır**
	h*ah*-yuhr
There isn't/aren't any . . .	**. . . yok**
	yohk
I'm sorry	**Özür dilerim**
	er-*zooh*r dee-leh-r*eem*
I don't have a list of campsites	**Kamp listesi yok**
	kahmp lees-teh-*see* yohk
I haven't got any left	**Kalmamış**
	k*ahl*-mah-muhsh
It's free	**Bedava**
	beh-d*ah*-vah

Accommodation

Hotel

ESSENTIAL INFORMATION

- If you want hotel-type accommodation, all the following words in capital letters are worth looking for on name boards:
  OTEL
  MOTEL
  PANSİYON (a small family hotel)
- A list of hotels in the town can usually be obtained at the local tourist office [see p. 22].
- Hotels are officially classified into five categories: luxury, then classes 1 to 4. Some medium-class hotels can be as good as, or even better than, those in higher categories.
- The cost is displayed in the room itself so you can check it when having a look around before agreeing to stay.
- The displayed cost is for the room itself, per night, and not per person. Breakfast is sometimes included. A Turkish breakfast consists of eggs, white cheese, olives, bread and jam or honey, with tea, coffee or milk.
- Service is included in the bill but tipping of the staff, especially after a long stay, is usual.
- Your passport is requested when registering.
- For finding a hotel, see p. 17.

WHAT TO SAY

I have a booking	**Rezervasyonum var**
	reh-zehr-vahs-yoh-n*oo*m vahr
Have you any rooms, please?	**Odanız var mı?**
	oh-dah-n*uh*z vahr muh
Can I book a room?	**Rezervasyon yapabiliyor muyum?**
	reh-zehr-vahs-yohn yah-pah-bee-*lee*-yohr muh-y*u*hm

For one person	**Tek kişilik**
	tehk kee-shee-*leek*
For two people	**İki kişilik**
	ee-k*ee* kee-shee-*leek*
[*For numbers, see p. 118*]	
For . . .	**. . . için**
	ee-ch*ee*n
one night	**Bir gece**
	beer gheh-j*eh*
two nights	**İki gece**
	ee-k*ee* gheh-j*eh*
one week	**Bir hafta**
	beer hahf-t*ah*
two weeks	**İki hafta**
	ee-k*ee* hahf-t*ah*
I would like . . .	**. . . istiyorum**
	ees-t*ee*-yoh-room
a room	**Bir oda**
	beer oh-d*ah*
two rooms	**İki oda**
	ee-k*ee* oh-d*ah*
with a single bed	**tek yataklı**
	tehk yah-tahk-l*uh*
with two single beds	**çift yataklı**
	cheeft yah-tahk-l*uh*
with a double bed	**iki kişilik yataklı**
	ee-k*ee* kee-shee-*leek* yah-tahk-l*uh*
with a toilet	**tuvaletli**
	too-wah-leht-l*ee*
with a bathroom	**banyolu**
	bahn-yoh-l*oo*
with a shower	**duşlu**
	doosh-l*oo*
with a cot	**çocuk yatağı ile**
	choh-j*oo*k yah-tah-*uh* ee-l*eh*
with a balcony	**balkonlu**
	bahl-kohn-l*oo*
Do you serve meals?	**Yemek servisi yapıyor musunuz?**
	yeh-m*eh*k sehr-vee-*see* yah-p*uh*-yohr moo-soo-n*oo*z
At what time is . . .	**Saat kaçta . . .**
	sah-*ah*t kahch-t*ah*

breakfast?	**kahvaltı?**
	kah-vahl-t*uh*
lunch?	**öğle yemeği?**
	er-leh yeh-meh-*ee*
dinner?	**akşam yemeği?**
	ahk-shahm yeh-meh-*ee*
How much is it?	**Ne kadar?**
	neh kah-d*ah*r
Can I look at the room?	**Odaya bakabilir miyim?**
	oh-d*ah*-yah bah-kah-bee-l*eer* mee-yeem
I'd prefer a room . . .	**. . . bir oda tercih ederim**
	beer oh-d*ah* tehr-jee eh-deh-r*ee*m
at the front/at the back	**Ön tarafta/Arka tarafta**
	ern tah-rahf-t*ah*/ahr-k*ah* tah-rahf-t*ah*
OK, I'll take it	**Tamam, bunu tutarım**
	tah-m*ah*m boo-n*oo* too-tah-r*uh*m
No thanks, I won't take it	**Teşekkürler, bunu istemiyorum**
	teh-shehk-koohr-lehr boo-n*oo* ees-teh-mee-yoh-room
The key to number (10), please	**Oda anahtarı, numara (on), lütfen**
	oh-d*ah* ah-nah-tah-r*uh* noo-mah-r*ah* (ohn) l*oo*ht-fehn
Please may I have . . .	**Lütfen, . . . veriniz**
	l*oo*ht-fehn . . . veh-ree-n*ee*z
a coat hanger	**bir askı**
	beer ahs-k*uh*
a towel	**bir havlu**
	bee hahv-l*oo*
a glass	**bir bardak**
	beer bahr-d*ah*k
some soap	**sabun**
	sah-b*oo*n
an ashtray	**bir küllük**
	beer koohl-l*oo*hk
another pillow	**bir yastık daha**
	beer yahs-t*uh*k dah-h*ah*
another blanket	**bir battaniye daha**
	beer baht-t*ah*-nee-yeh dah-h*ah*
Come in!	**Buyurun!**
	boo-yoo-r*oo*n

One moment, please	**Bir dakika, lütfen**
	beer dah-kee-kah looht-fehn
Please (would you) . . .	**Lütfen . . .**
	looht-fehn
do this laundry	**bu çamaşırı yıkayınız**
	boo chah-mah-shuh-ruh yah-kah-yuh-nuhz
do this dry cleaning	**bunu kuru temizlemeye veriniz**
	boo-noo koo-roo teh-meez-leh-meh-yeh veh-ree-neez
call me at (6) o'clock	**saat (altı) da bana haber veriniz**
	sah-aht (ahl-tuh) dah bah-nah hah-behr veh-ree-neez
help me with my luggage	**bagajıma yardım ediniz**
	bah-gah-zhuh-mah yahr-duhm eh-dee-neez
call me a taxi for (7) o'clock	**saat (yedi) için bir taksi cağırınız**
	sah-aht (yeh-dee) ee-cheen beer tahk-see chah-uh-ruh-nuhz
[For times, see p. 120]	
The bill, please	**Hesabı, lütfen**
	heh-sah-buh looht-fehn
Is service included?	**Servis dahil mi?**
	sehr-vees dah-heel mee
I think this is wrong	**Bir yanlışlık var galiba**
	beer yahn-luhsh-luhk vahr gah-lee-bah
May I have a receipt	**Bir makbuz veriniz**
	beer mahk-booz veh-ree-neez

At breakfast

Some more . . . please	**Biraz daha . . . lütfen**
	bee-rahz dah-hah . . . looht-fehn
coffee	**kahve**
	kah-veh
tea	**çay**
	chay
bread	**ekmek**
	ehk-mehk
butter	**tereyağ**
	teh-reh-yah

jam/honey	**reçel/bal** reh-ch*eh*l/bahl
A boiled egg, please	**Bir kaynamış yumurta, lütfen** beer kay-nah-m*uh*sh yoo-moor-t*ah* *loo*ht-fehn

LIKELY REACTIONS

Have you an identity document, please?	**Hüviyetiniz var mı, lütfen?** hooh-vee-yeh-tee-n*eez* vahr muh *loo*ht-fehn
What's your name?	**Adınız ne?** ah-duh-n*uh*z neh
Sorry, we're full	**Özür dilerim, doluyuz** er-z*oo*hr dee-leh-r*ee*m doh-loo- *yoo*z
We have no rooms	**Odamız yok** oh-dah-m*uh*z yohk
Do you want to have a look?	**Bakmak ister misiniz?** Bahk-m*ah*k ees-t*eh*r mee-see-n*eez*
How many people is it for?	**Kaç kişi için** kahch kee-sh*ee* ee-ch*ee*n
From (7) o'clock onwards	**Saat (yedi)den sonra** sah-*ah*t (yeh-dee)d*eh*n s*oh*n-rah
From (midday) onwards	**(Öğleden) sonra** (er-leh-d*eh*n) s*oh*n-rah
[*For times, see p. 120*] It's (10,000) lira	**(On bin) lira** (ohn been) l*ee*-rah
[*For numbers, see p. 118*]	

Camping and youth hostelling

ESSENTIAL INFORMATION

Camping .

• Look for the words **KAMP** or **CAMPING** and signs like these:

- Be prepared to have to pay
  per person
  for the car (if applicable)
  for the tent or caravan plot
  for electricity
  for hot showers
- You must provide proof of identity, such as your passport.
- You can obtain information on campsites from local tourist offices.
- There are camping sites throughout Turkey, including some good ones in or near the main cities and tourist attractions. Camping off site is also possible, though one should try to ask permission of the landowner. Camping in very remote places is not advisable.

Youth hostels

- Because of the general availability of low-cost accommodation there are few hostels in Turkey. Those that do exist are essentially student hostels with shared facilities. None of them requires an IYHF (International Youth Hostel Federation) card, though some offer cardholders 10–20% discounts.

WHAT TO SAY

I have a booking	**Rezervasyonum var**
	reh-zehr-vahs-yoh-noom vahr
Have you any space?	**Boş yeriniz var mı?**
	bohsh yeh-ree-neez vahr muh
It's for . . .	**. . . için**
	ee-cheen
one person	**Bir tek kişi**
	beer tehk kee-shee
two people	**İki kişi**
	ee-kee kee-shee
and one child	**ve bir çocuk**
	veh beer choh-jook
and two children	**ve iki çocuk**
	veh ee-kee choh-jook
It's for . . .	**. . . için**
	ee-cheen
one night	**Bir tek gece**
	beer tehk gheh-jeh
two nights	**İki gece**
	ee-kee gheh-jeh

one week	**Bir hafta**
	beer hahf-t*a*h
two weeks	**İki hafta**
	ee-k*ee* hahf-t*a*h
How much is it . . .	**. . . ne kadar?**
	neh kah-d*a*hr
for the tent?	**Çadır**
	chah-d*u*hr
for the caravan?	**Karavan**
	kah-rah-v*a*hn
for the car?	**Araba**
	ah-rah-b*a*h
for the electricity?	**Elektrik**
	eh-lehk-tr*ee*k
per person?	**Kişi için**
	kee-sh*ee* ee-ch*ee*n
per night?	**Gece için**
	gheh-ch*e*h ee-ch*ee*n
May I look round?	**Bakabilir miyim?**
	bah-kah-bee-l*ee*r mee-y*ee*m
At what time do you lock up at night?	**Saat kaçta kapayı kilitliyorsunuz?**
	sah-*a*ht kahch-t*a*h kah-pah-y*u*h kee-leet-lee-yohr-soo-n*oo*z
Is there anything . . .	**. . . var mı?**
	vahr muh
to eat?	**Yemek**
	yeh-m*e*hk
to drink?	**İçecek**
	ee-ch*e*h-jehk
Is/are there . . .	**. . . var mı?**
	vahr muh
a bar?	**Bar**
	bahr
hot showers?	**Sıcak duşlar**
	suh-j*a*hk doosh-l*a*hr
a kitchen?	**Mutfak**
	moot-f*a*hk
a laundry?	**Çamaşırhane**
	chah-mah-sh*u*hr-hah-neh
a restaurant?	**Lokanta**
	loh-k*a*hn-tah

a shop?	**Dükkân**
	doohk-k*a*hn
a swimming pool?	**Yüzme havuzu**
	yoohz-m*e*h hah-voo-z*oo*

[*For food shopping, see p. 53, and for eating and drinking out, see p. 72*]

Where are . . .   **. . . nerede?**
neh-reh-d*e*h

the dustbins?	**Çöp kutuları**
	cherp koo-too-lah-r*u*h
the showers?	**Duşlar**
	doosh-l*a*hr
the toilets?	**Tuvaletler**
	too-wah-leht-l*e*hr

Please have you got . . .   **Lütfen . . . var mı?**
l*oo*ht-fehn . . . vahr muh

a broom?	**süpürge**
	sooh-poohr-gh*e*h
a corkscrew?	**tirbuşon**
	teer-boo-sh*o*hn
a drying-up cloth?	**kurulama bezi**
	koo-roo-lah-m*a*h beh-z*ee*
a fork?	**çatal**
	chah-t*a*hl
a fridge?	**buzdolabı**
	booz-doh-lah-b*u*h
a frying pan?	**tava**
	tah-v*a*h
an iron?	**ütü**
	ooh-t*oo*h
a knife?	**bıçak**
	buh-ch*a*hk
a plate?	**tabak**
	tah-b*a*hk
a saucepan?	**tencere**
	t*e*hn-jeh-reh
a teaspoon?	**çay kaşığı**
	chay kah-shuh-*u*h
a tin-opener?	**konserve açacağı**
	kohn-s*e*hr-veh ah-chah-jah-*u*h
washing powder?	**çamaşır tozu**
	chah-mah-sh*u*hr toh-z*oo*

washing-up liquid?	**bulaşık deterjanı**
	boo-lah-sh*u*hk deh-tehr-jah-n*u*h
The bill, please	**Hesabı, lütfen**
	heh-sah-b*u*h l*oo*ht-fehn

Problems

The toilet	**Tuvalet**
	too-wah-l*e*ht
The shower	**Duş**
	doosh
The tap	**Musluk**
	moos-l*oo*k
The razor point	**Traş makinası için priz**
	trahsh mah-kee-nah-s*u*h ee-ch*ee*n preez
The light	**Işık**
	uh-sh*u*hk
. . . is not working	**. . . yanmıyor**
	y*a*hn-muh-yohr
My camping gas has run out	**Bütan gazım bitmiş**
	booh-tahn gah-z*u*hm beet-m*ee*sh

LIKELY REACTIONS

Have you an identity document, please?	**Hüviyetiniz var mı, lütfen?**
	hooh-vee-yeh-tee-n*ee*z vahr muh l*oo*ht-fehn
What's your name?	**Adınız ne?**
	ah-duh-n*u*hz neh
Sorry, we're full	**Özür dilerim, doluyuz**
	er-z*oo*hr dee-leh-r*ee*m doh-loo-y*oo*z
How many people is it for?	**Kaç kişi için**
	kahch kee-sh*ee* ee-ch*ee*n
How many nights is it for?	**Kaç gece için**
	kahch gheh-jeh ee-ch*ee*n
It's (8,000) lira	**(Sekiz bin) lira**
	(seh-k*ee*z been) l*ee*-rah

[*For numbers, see p. 118*]

Rented accommodation: problem solving

ESSENTIAL INFORMATION

- If you are looking for accommodation to rent, look out for these
  words:
  KİRALIK (for rent)
  APARTMAN DAİRESİ (apartment, flat)
- For arranging your let, see 'Hotel', p. 24.
- Key words you will meet if renting on the spot:
  Depozito (deposit)
  deh-poh-*zee*-toh
  Anahtar (key)
  ah-nah-*ta*hr
- Having arranged your own accommodation and arrived with the
  key, check the obvious basics that you take for granted at home.
  Electricity: voltage? Usually the supply is 240v, but there are some
  districts where it is 110v, so razors and small appliances brought
  from home may need adjusting. For razors and appliances with
  three-point plugs it is well worth bringing adaptors from home to
  fit the two-point continental sockets that are universal.
  Cooker: there may not be an oven, and don't be surprised to find:
  – a lid covering the rings which lifts up to form a splashback
  – a mixture of gas and electric rings.
  Toilet: Turkish plumbing blocks easily, so do not throw things in
  the toilet. Some toilets cannot take toilet paper – if so a bin is
  provided beside the lavatory to dispose of it.
  Water: find the stopcock. Check taps and plugs – they may not
  operate in the way you are used to. Check how to turn on (or
  light) the hot water.
  Windows: check the method of opening and closing the windows
  and shutters.
  Insects: is an insecticide spray provided? If not, get one locally.
  Equipment: for buying or replacing equipment, see p. 48.
- You will probably have an official agent, but be clear in your own
  mind whom to contact in an emergency, even if it is only a
  neighbour in the first place.

WHAT TO SAY

My name is . . .	**Adım . . .** ah-du*h*m
I'm staying at . . .	**. . . 'da kalıyorum** . . . dah kah-l*uh*-yoh-room
The . . . has been cut off	**. . . kesilmiş** keh-seel-m*ee*sh
electricity	**Elektrik** eh-lehk-tr*eek*
gas	**Havagazı** hah-v*ah*-gah-zuh
water	**Su** soo
Is there . . . in the area?	**Civarda . . . var mı?** jee-vahr-d*ah* . . . vahr muh
an electrician	**elektrikçi** eh-lehk-treek-ch*ee*
a plumber	**borucu** boh-roo-j*oo*
a gas fitter	**havagazı ustası** hah-v*ah*-gah-zuh oos-tah-s*uh*
Where is . . .	**. . . nerede?** neh-reh-d*eh*
the fusebox?	**Sigorta** see-g*oh*r-tah
the stopcock? (water main)	**Su vanası** soo vah-nah-s*uh*
the boiler?	**Kazan** kah-z*ah*n
the (electric) water heater?	**Termosifon** tehr-moh-see-f*oh*n
Is there . . .	**. . . var mı?** vahr muh
town gas?	**Havagazı** hah-v*ah*-gah-zuh
bottled gas?	**Bütan gazı** boo-t*ah*n gah-z*uh*
central heating?	**Kalorifer** kah-loh-ree-f*eh*r
The cooker	**Ocak** oh-j*ah*k

The hair dryer	**Saç kurutma makinası** sahch koo-roo-too-m*a*h mah-kee-nah-s*u*h
The heating	**Kalorifer** kah-loh-ree-f*e*hr
The immersion heater	**Termosifon** tehr-moh-see-f*o*hn
The iron	**Ütü** ooh-t*o*oh
The pilot light	**Pilot** pee-l*o*ht
The refrigerator	**Buzdolabı** booz-doh-lah-b*u*h
The telephone	**Telefon** teh-leh-f*o*hn
The washing machine	**Çamaşır makinası** chah-mah-sh*u*hr mah-kee-nah-s*u*h
The (electric) water heater	**Termosifon** tehr-moh-see-f*o*hn
. . . is not working	**. . . işlemiyor** ish-l*e*h-mee-yohr
Where can I get . . .	**. . . nerede bulabilirim?** neh-reh-d*e*h boo-lah-bee-lee-r*e*em
an adaptor for this?	**Bunun için bir adaptör** boo-n*oo*n ee-ch*ee*n beer ah-dahp-ter
a bottle of butane gas?	**Bir tüp bütan gazı** beer toohp booh-t*a*hn gah-z*u*h
a fuse?	**Bir sigorta** beer see-g*oh*r-tah
an insecticide spray?	**Böcek öldürücüsü** ber-j*e*hk erl-dooh-rooh-jooh-s*oo*h
a light bulb?	**Bir ampul** beer ahm-p*oo*l
The drain	**Pis su borusu** pees soo boh-ruh-s*oo*
The sink	**Eviye** eh-vee-y*e*h
The toilet	**Tuvalet** too-wah-l*e*ht
. . . is blocked	**. . . tıkalı** tuh-kah-l*u*h

The gas is leaking

Gazı kaçak yapıyor
gah-z*uh* kah-ch*a*hk yah-p*uh*-yohr

Can you mend it straightaway?

Hemen tamir edebilir misiniz?
heh-m*e*hn tah-m*ee*r eh-deh-bee-l*ee*r
mee-see-n*ee*z

When can you mend it?

Ne zaman tamir edebilir siniz?
neh zah-m*a*hn tah-m*ee*r eh-deh-
bee-l*ee*r see-n*ee*z

How much do I owe you?

Borcum ne kadar?
bohr-j*oo*m neh kah-d*a*hr

When is the rubbish collected?

Çöp ne zaman toplanıyor?
cherp neh zah-m*a*hn toh-plah-n*uh*-
yohr

LIKELY REACTIONS

What's your name?

Adınız ne?
ah-duh-n*uh*z neh

What's your address?

Adresiniz ne?
ah-dreh-see-n*ee*z neh

There's a shop . . .

. . . dükkân var
doohk-k*a*hn vahr

in town

Şehirde
sheh-heer-d*e*h

in the village

Köyde
ker-yee-d*e*h

I can't come . . .

. . . gelemiyorum
gheh-l*e*h-mee-yoh-room

today

Bugün
boo-g*oo*hn

this week

Bu hafta
boo hahf-t*a*h

until Monday

Pazartesinden önce
pah-zahr-teh-seen-d*e*hn ern-jeh

I can come . . .

. . . gelebiliyorum
gheh-leh-bee-l*ee*-yoh-room

on Tuesday

Salı günü
sah-l*uh* gooh-n*oo*h

when you want

Her ne zaman isterseniz
hehr neh zah-m*a*hn ees-tehr-seh-
n*ee*z

Every day	**Her gün**
	hehr goohn
Every other day	**İki günde bir**
	ee-k*ee* goohn-d*e*h beer
On Wednesdays	**Çarşamba günleri**
	chahr-shahm-b*a*h goohn-leh-r*ee*

[*For days of the week, see p. 122*]

General shopping

The chemist's

ESSENTIAL INFORMATION

- Look out for this word:
  ECZANE (chemist)
  NÖBETÇİ ECZANE (duty chemist)
- Chemists are easy to find, open until about 8.00 p.m., and in each district take it in turns to stay open throughout the night and during holidays. The name and address of the nearest duty chemist is displayed in the window of every chemist shop.
- Many drugs available only on prescription in the UK can be bought over the counter in Turkey.
- For finding a chemist, see p. 17.

WHAT TO SAY

I'd like . . .	**. . . istiyorum**
	ees-*tee*-yoh-room
some aspirin	**Aspirin**
	ahs-pee-r*ee*n

some antiseptic	**Antiseptik**
	ahn-tee-sehp-*teek*
some bandage	**Sargı**
	sahr-g*u*h
some cotton wool	**Pamuk**
	pah-m*oo*k
some eye drops	**Göz damlası**
	gherz dahm-lah-s*u*h
some foot powder	**Ayak pudrası**
	ah-yahk poo-drah-s*u*h
some gauze dressing	**Gazlı bez**
	gahz-l*u*h behz
some inhalant	**İnhalatör**
	een-hah-lah-t*er*
some insect repellent	**Böcek kremi**
	ber-jehk kreh-m*ee*
some lip salve	**Dudak kremi**
	doo-d*a*hk kreh-m*ee*
some nose drops	**Burun damlası**
	boo-r*oo*n dahm-lah-s*u*h
some sticking plaster	**Plaster**
	plah-st*ehr*
some throat pastilles	**Boğaz pastili**
	boh-*a*hz pahs-tee-l*ee*
some Vaseline	**Vazelin**
	vah-zeh-l*ee*n
I'd like something for . . .	**. . . için bir şey istiyorum**
	ee-ch*ee*n beer shey ees-*tee*-yoh-room
(insect) bites	**Böcek ısırığı**
	ber-jehk uh-suh-ruh-*u*h
burns	**Yanık**
	yah-n*u*hk
chilblains	**Mayasıl**
	mah-yah-s*u*hl
a cold	**Nezle**
	nehz-leh
constipation	**Kabızlık**
	kah-buhz-l*u*hk
a cough	**Öksürük**
	erk-sooh-r*oo*hk
diarrhoea	**İshal**
	ees-h*a*hl

earache	**Kulak ağrısı**
	koo-l*a*hk ah-ruh-s*u*h
flu	**Grip**
	greep
scalds	**Yanık**
	yah-n*u*hk
sore gums	**Dişeti ağrısı**
	deesh-eh-t*ee* ah-ruh-s*u*h
sprains	**Burkulma**
	boor-kool-m*a*h
stings	**Sokma**
	sohk-m*a*h
sunburn	**Güneş yanığı**
	gooh-nehsh yah-nuh-*u*h
car/sea/air/travel sickness	**Araba/Deniz/Hava/Yol tutması**
	ah-rah-b*a*h/deh-n*ee*z/hah-v*a*h/yohl toot-mah-s*u*h
I need . . .	**. . . istiyorum**
	ees-t*ee*-yoh-room
some baby food	**Mama**
	mah-m*a*h
some contraceptives	**Preservatif**
	preh-sehr-vah-t*ee*f
some deodorant	**Deodoran**
	deh-oh-doh-r*a*hn
some (disposable) nappies	**Çocuk bezi**
	choh-j*oo*k beh-z*ee*
some hand cream	**El kremi**
	ehl kreh-m*ee*
some lipstick	**Ruj**
	roozh
some make-up remover	**Makyaj silme**
	mahk-y*a*hzh seel-meh
some paper tissues	**Kağıt mendil**
	kah-*u*ht mehn-d*ee*l
some razor blades	**Tıraş bıçağı**
	tuh-r*a*hsh buh-chah-*u*h
some safety pins	**Çengelli iğne**
	chehn-ghehl-l*ee* ee-neh
some sanitary towels	**Hijenik bez**
	hee-zheh-n*ee*k behz
some shaving cream	**Tıraş kremi**
	tuh-r*a*hsh kreh-m*ee*

some soap	**Sabun**
	sah-b*oo*n
some suntan lotion/oil	**Güneş kremi/yağı**
	gooh-n*e*hsh kreh-m*ee*/yah-*u*h
some talcum powder	**Talk pudrası**
	tahlk poo-drah-s*u*h
some Tampax	**Tampaks**
	tahm-p*a*hks
some toilet paper	**Tuvalet kağıdı**
	too-wah-l*e*ht kah-uh-d*u*h
some toothpaste	**Diş macunu**
	deesh mah-joo-n*oo*

[*For other essential expressions, see 'Shop talk', p. 50*]

Holiday items

ESSENTIAL INFORMATION

- Places to shop at and signs to look for:
  FOTOĞRAFÇI (photographer)
  KIRTASİYECİ (stationer)
  KİTABEVİ (bookshop)
  TÜTÜNCÜ (tobacconist)

WHAT TO SAY

Where can I buy . . .	. . . **nerede alabiliyorum?**
	neh-reh-d*e*h ah-lah-bee-l*ee*-yoh-room
a bag?	**Bir çanta**
	beer ch*a*hn-tah
a beach ball?	**Plaj için bir top**
	plahzh ee-ch*ee*n beer tohp
a bucket?	**Bir kova**
	beer koh-v*a*h

an English newspaper?	**İngilizce gazete**
	een-ghee-*lee*z-jeh gah-*zeh*-teh
some envelopes?	**Zarf**
	zahrf
a guide book?	**Bir rehber**
	beer reh-*beh*r
a map?	**Bir harita**
	beer hah-*ree*-tah
some postcards?	**Kartpostal**
	kahrt-pohs-*tah*l
a spade?	**Bir bel**
	beer behl
a straw hat?	**Bir hasır şapka**
	beer hah-s*u*hr shahp-k*a*h
a suitcase?	**Bir valiz**
	beer vah-*lee*z
some sunglasses?	**Güneş gözlüğü**
	gooh-n*e*hsh gerz-looh-*ooh*
a sunshade?	**Bir şemsiye**
	beer sh*e*hm-see-yeh
some writing paper?	**Yazı kâğıdı**
	yah-z*u*h kah-uh-d*u*h
I'd like . . . [*show the camera*]	**. . . istiyorum**
	ees-t*ee*-yoh-room
a colour film	**Renkli filim**
	rehn-kl*ee* fee-*lee*m
a black and white film	**Siyah-beyaz filim**
	see-yah-beh-y*a*hz fee-l*ee*m
for prints	**baskı için**
	bahs-k*u*h ee-ch*ee*n
for slides	**slayt için**
	slahyt ee-ch*ee*n
12(24/36) exposures	**on iki (yirmi dört/otuz altı) pozluk**
	ohn ee-k*ee* (yeer-m*ee* derrt/oh-t*ooz* ahl-t*u*h) pohz-l*oo*k
a standard 8mm film	**Standart sekiz milimetrelik filim**
	stahn-d*a*hrt seh-k*ee*z mee-lee-meh-treh-l*ee*k fee-l*ee*m
a super 8 film	**Süper sekizlik filim**
	sooh-p*e*hr seh-keez-l*ee*k fee-l*ee*m
some flash bulbs	**Flaş lambası**
	flahsh lahm-bah-s*u*h

This camera is broken	**Bu fotoğraf makinası bozuk** boo foh-toh-r*a*hf mah-kee-nah-s*u*h boh-z*oo*k
The film is stuck	**Filim takıldı** fee-l*ee*m tah-kuhl-d*u*h
Please can you . . .	**Lütfen . . .** l*oo*ht-fehn
develop this?	**develop edebilir misiniz?** deh-veh-l*o*hp eh-deh-bee-l*ee*r mee- see-n*ee*z
print this	**basabilir misiniz?** bah-sah-bee-l*ee*r mee-see-n*ee*z
load the camera	**filim makinaya koyabilir misiniz?** fee-l*ee*m mah-kee-nah-y*a*h koh- yah-bee-l*ee*r mee-see-n*ee*z

[*For other essential expressions, see 'Shop talk', p. 50*]

The tobacconist's

ESSENTIAL INFORMATION

- The sign for tobacconists in Turkey is:
  TÜTÜNCÜ
- Tobacconists often sell newspapers, wine and spirits.
- Cigarettes can also be bought from street vendors.

WHAT TO SAY

A packet of cigarettes	**. . . bir paket sigara** beer pah-k*e*ht see-g*a*h-rah
with filters	**Filtreli** feel-treh-l*ee*
without filters	**Filtresiz** feel-treh-s*ee*z
menthol	**Mentollü** mehn-tohl-l*oo*

A packet of kingsize cigarettes	**Bir paket uzun sigara**
	beer pah-keht oo-zoon see-gah-rah
Those up there . . .	**Şu üsttekileri . . .**
	shoo oohst-teh-kee-leh-ree
on the right	**sağda**
	sah-dah
on the left	**solda**
	sohl-dah
These [point]	**Şunlar**
	shoon-lahr
Cigarettes, please	**Sigara, lütfen**
	see-gah-rah looht-fehn
100/200/300	**Yüz/iki yüz/üç yüz**
	yoohz/ee-kee yoohz/oohch yoohz
Two packets	**İki paket**
	ee-kee pah-keht
Have you got . . .	**. . . var mı?**
	vahr muh
English cigarettes?	**İngiliz sigarası**
	een-ghee-leez see-gah-rah-suh
American cigarettes?	**Amerikan sigarası**
	ah-meh-ree-kahn see-gah-rah-suh
English pipe tobacco	**İngiliz pipo tütünü**
	een-ghee-leez pee-poh tooh-tooh-nooh
American pipe tobacco	**Amerikan pipo tütünü**
	ah-meh-ree-kahn pee-poh tooh-tooh-nooh
A packet of pipe tobacco	**Bir paket pipo tütünü**
	beer pah-keht pee-poh tooh-tooh-nooh
That one up there . . .	**Şu üsttekini . . .**
	shoo oohst-teh-kee-nee
on the right	**sağda**
	sah-dah
on the left	**solda**
	sohl-dah
That one [point]	**Şu**
	shoo
A cigar, please	**Bir puro**
	beer poo-roh
This one [point]	**Bu**
	booh

Some cigars, please	**Birkaç puro, lütfen**
	beer-kahch poo-roh looht-fehn
Those [point]	**Onlar**
	ohn-lahr
A box of matches	**Kibrit**
	kee-breet
A packet of pipe cleaners	**Bir paket pipo temizleyicisi**
	beer pah-keht pee-poh teh-meez-leh-yee-jee-see
A packet of flints [show lighter]	**Bir paket çakmak taşı**
	beer pah-keht chahk-mahk tah-shuh
Lighter fuel	**Çakmak benzini**
	chahk-mahk behn-zee-nee
Lighter gas, please	**Çakmak gazı, lütfen**
	chahk-mahk gah-zuh looht-fehn

[For other essential expressions, see 'Shop talk', p. 50]

Buying clothes

ESSENTIAL INFORMATION

- Look for:
  ELBİSE (clothing)
  GİYİM (clothing)
  GİYİMEVİ (clothing store)
- Don't buy without being measured first or without trying things on.
- Don't rely on conversion charts of clothing sizes [see p. 133].
- If you are buying for someone else, take their measurements with you.

WHAT TO SAY

I'd like . . .	. . . **istiyorum**
	ees-tee-yoh-room

an anorak	**Bir parka**
	beer pahr-k*a*h
a belt	**Bir kemer**
	beer keh-m*e*hr
a bikini	**Bir bikini**
	beer bee-kee-n*ee*
a bra	**Bir sutyen**
	beer soot-y*e*hn
a bathing cap	**Bir bone**
	beer boh-n*e*h
a cardigan	**Bir hırka**
	beer huhr-k*a*h
a coat	**Bir palto**
	beer pahl-t*o*h
a dress	**Bir elbise**
	beer ehl-bee-s*e*h
a hat	**Bir şapka**
	beer shahp-k*a*h
a jacket	**Bir ceket**
	beer jeh-k*e*ht
a jumper	**Bir kazak**
	beer kah-z*a*hk
a nightdress	**Bir gecelik**
	beer gheh-jeh-l*ee*k
a pullover	**Bir kazak**
	beer kah-z*a*hk
some pyjamas	**Bir pijama**
	beer pee-j*a*h-mah
a raincoat	**Bir yağmurluk**
	beer yah-moor-l*oo*k
a shirt [*for a woman*]	**Bir bluz**
	beer blooz
a shirt [*for a man*]	**Bir gömlek**
	beer gherm-l*e*hk
a skiing cap	**Bir ski şapkası**
	beer skee shahp-kah-s*u*h
a skirt	**Bir etek**
	beer eh-t*e*hk
a suit [*for a woman*]	**Bir tayör**
	beer tah-y*e*r
a suit [*for a man*]	**Bir kostüm**
	beer kohs-t*oo*hm

a swimsuit	**Bir mayo**
	beer mah-yoh
some tights	**Bir külotlu çorap**
	beer kooh-loht-loo choh-rahp
some trousers	**Bir pantalon**
	beer pahn-tah-lohn
a T-shirt	**Bir tişort**
	beer tee-shohrt
I'd like . . .	**. . . istiyorum**
	ees-tee-yoh-room
a pair of briefs [for a woman]	**Bir külot**
	beer kooh-loht
a pair of gloves	**Eldivenler**
	ehl-dee-vehn-lehr
a pair of jeans	**Bir blucin**
	beer bloo-jeen
a pair of shorts	**Bir şort**
	beer shohrt
a pair of underpants [for a man]	**Bir külot**
	beer kooh-loht
I'd like a pair of . . .	**Bir çift . . . istiyorum**
	beer cheeft . . . ees-tee-yoh-room
(short/long) socks	**(kısa/uzun) çorap**
	(kuh-sah/oo-zoon) choh-rahp
stockings	**kadın çorabı**
	kah-duhn choh-rah-buh
shoes	**ayakkabı**
	ah-yahk-kah-buh
canvas shoes	**tenis ayakkabısı**
	teh-nees ah-yahk-kah-buh-suh
sandals	**sandal**
	sahn-dahl
boots	**çizme**
	cheez-meh
moccasins	**mokasen**
	moh-kah-sehn
slippers	**terlik**
	tehr-leek
I'd like a pair of beach shoes	**Plaj için bir çift ayakkabı istiyorum**
	plahzh ee-cheen beer cheeft ah-yahk-ah-buh ees-tee-yoh-room

The size is . . .	**. . . numarası** noo-mah-rah-s*uh*
[*For numbers, see p. 118*]	
Can you measure me, please?	**Ölçülerimi alır mısınız, lütfen?** erl-chooh-leh-ree-m*ee* ah-l*uh*r muh-suh-n*uh*z l*oo*ht-fehn
Can I try it on?	**Bunu deneyebilir miyim?** boo-n*oo* deh-neh-yeh-bee-l*ee*r mee-y*ee*m
It's for a present	**Hediye olarak** heh-dee-yeh oh-lah-r*ah*k
These are the measurements	**İşte ölçüleri**
[*show written*]	eesh-t*eh* erl-chooh-leh-r*ee*
bust	**büst** boohst
chest	**göğüs** gher-*oo*hs
collar	**yaka** yah-k*ah*
hip	**kalça** kahl-ch*ah*
leg	**bacak** bah-j*ah*k
waist	**bel** behl
Have you got something . . .	**. . . bir şeyiniz var mı?** beer sheh-yee-n*eez* vahr muh
in black?	**Siyah** see-y*ah*
in grey?	**Gri** gree
in blue?	**Mavi** mah-v*ee*
in brown?	**Kahverengi** kah-v*eh*-rehn-ghee
in pink?	**Pembe** pehm-b*eh*
in green?	**Yeşil** yeh-sh*eel*
in red?	**Kırmızı** kuhr-muh-z*uh*

in yellow?	**Sarı**
	sah-ruh
in this colour?	**Bu renkte**
	boo rehnk-teh
in cotton?	**Pamuklu**
	pah-mook-loo
in denim?	**Blucin kumaşı**
	bloo-jeen koo-mah-shuh
in leather?	**Deri**
	deh-ree
in nylon?	**Naylon**
	nay-lohn
in suede?	**Süet**
	sooh-eht
in wool?	**Yünlü**
	yoohn-looh
in this material?	**Bu kumaştan**
	boo koo-mahsh-tahn

[*For other essential expressions, see 'Shop talk', p. 50*]

Replacing equipment

ESSENTIAL INFORMATION

- Look for these shop signs:
  ELEKTRİKÇİ (electrician)
  HIRDAVATÇI (ironmonger)
  NALBUR (ironmonger)
  SÜPERMARKET (supermarket)
- To ask the way to the shop, see p. 17.

WHAT TO SAY

Have you got . . .	. . . **var mı?**
	vahr muh
an adaptor? [*show appliance*]	**Bir adaptör**
	beer ah-dahp-ter

a bottle of butane gas?	**Bir tüp bütan gazı** beer toop booh-tahn gah-zuh
a bottle opener?	**Bir şişe açacağı** beer shee-sheh ah-chah-jah-uh
a corkscrew?	**Bir tirbuşon** beer teer-boo-shohn
any disinfectant?	**Dezenfektan** deh-zehn-fehk-tahn
any paper/plastic cups?	**Kâğıt/plastik fincan** kah-uht/plahs-teek feen-jahn
any paper/plastic plates?	**Kâğıt/plastik tabak** kah-uht/plahs-teek tah-bahk
a drying-up cloth?	**Bir kurulama bezi** beer koo-roo-lah-mah beh-zee
any forks	**Çatallar** chah-tahl-lahr
a fuse? [*show an old one*]	**Bir sigorta** beer see-gohr-tah
an insecticide spray?	**Böcek öldürücüsü** ber-jehk erl-dooh-rooh-jooh-sooh
a kitchen roll? [*paper*]	**Mutfak kâğıdı** moot-fahk kah-uh-duh
any knives?	**Bıçaklar** buh-cahk-lahr
a light bulb [*show old one*]	**Bir ampul** beer ahm-pool
a plastic bucket?	**Bir plastik kova** beer plahs-teek koh-vah
a plug (for the sink)?	**Bir tıkaç (eviye için)** beer tuh-kahch (eh-vee-yeh ee-cheen)
a spanner?	**Bir anahtar** beer ah-nah-tahr
a sponge?	**Bir sünger** beer soohn-ghehr
any string?	**İp** eep
any tent pegs?	**Çadır kazığı** chah-duhr kah-zuh-uh
a tin opener?	**Konserve açacağı** kohn-sehr-veh ah-chah-jah-uh
a torch?	**Bir elfeneri** beer ehl-feh-neh-ree

any (torch) batteries?	**Pil (elfeneri için)**
	peel (ehl-feh-neh-r*ee* ee-ch*ee*n)
a washing line?	**Bir çamaşır ipi**
	beer chah-mah-sh*u*hr ee-p*ee*
any washing powder?	**Çamaşır tozu**
	chah-mah-sh*u*hr toh-z*oo*
a washing-up brush?	**Bir bulaşık fırçası**
	beer boo-lah-sh*u*hk fuhr-chah-s*u*h
any washing-up liquid?	**Bulaşık deterjanı**
	boo-lah-sh*u*hk deh-tehr-jah-n*u*h

[*For other essential expressions, see 'Shop talk', below*]

Shop talk

ESSENTIAL INFORMATION

Know your coins and notes:
coins: 25, 50, 100 Turkish lira (TL)
notes: 100, 500, 1,000, 5,000, 10,000, 20,000.
- Know how to say the important weights and measures:

50 grams	**Elli gram**
	ehl-l*ee* grahm
100 grams	**Yüz gram**
	yoohz gram
200 grams	**İki yüz gram**
	ee-k*ee* yoohz grahm
½ kilo	**Yarım kilo**
	yah-r*u*hm kee-l*oh*
1 kilo	**Bir kilo**
	beer kee-l*oh*
2 kilos	**İki kilo**
	ee-k*ee* kee-loh
½ litre	**Yarım litre**
	yah-r*u*hm l*ee*-treh
1 litre	**Bir litre**
	beer l*ee*-treh
2 litres	**İki litre**
	ee-k*ee* l*ee*-treh

[*For numbers, see p. 118*]

CUSTOMER

Hello	**Merhaba** mehr-hah-bah
Good morning	**Günaydın** gooh-nay-duhn
Good day	**İyi günler** ee-yee goohn-lehr
Goodbye [*person staying*]	**Güle güle** gooh-leh gooh-leh
Goodbye [*person leaving*]	**Allahaısmarladık** ahl-lahs-mahr-lah-duhk
I'm just looking	**Sadece bakıyorum** sah-deh-jeh bah-kuh-yoh-room
Excuse me	**Affedersiniz** ahf-feh-dehr-see-neez
How much is this/that?	**Bu/şu ne kadar?** boo/shoo neh kah-dahr
What's that?	**Şu ne?** shoo neh
What are those?	**Şunlar ne?** shoon-lahr neh
Is there a discount?	**İskonto var mı?** ees-kohn-toh vahr muh
I'd like that, please	**Şunu istiyorum, lütfen** shoo-noo ees-tee-yoh-room looht-fehn
Not that	**Şunu değil** shoo-noo deh-eel
Like that	**Şunun gibi** shoo-noon gee-bee
That's enough, thank you	**O kadar yeter, teşekkür ederim** oh kah-dahr yeh-tehr teh-shehk-koohr eh-deh-reem
More, please	**Daha, lütfen** dah-hah looht-fehn
Less than that	**Ondan daha az** ohn-dahn dah-hah ahz
That's fine ⎤ OK	**Tamam** tah-mahm
I won't take it, thank you	**Almıyorum, teşekkür ederim** ahl-muh-yoh-room teh-shehk-koohr eh-deh-reem

It's not right	**Doğru değil**
	doh-*roo* deh-*ee*l
Thank you very much	**Çok teşekkür ederim**
	chohk teh-shehk-k*oo*hr eh-deh-*reem*
Is there something . . .	**. . . bir şey var mı?**
	beer shehy vahr muh
better?	**Daha iyi**
	dah-h*ah* ee-y*ee*
cheaper?	**Daha ucuz**
	dah-h*ah* oo-j*ooz*
different?	**Başka**
	bahsh-k*ah*
larger?	**Daha büyük**
	dah-h*ah* booh-y*oo*hk
smaller?	**Daha küçük**
	dah-hah kooh-ch*oo*hk
At what time . . .	**Saat kaçta . . .**
	sah-*ah*t kahch-t*ah*
do you open?	**açıyor sunuz?**
	ah-ch*uh*-yohr soo-n*ooz*
do you close?	**kapatıyor sunuz?**
	kah-pah-t*uh*-yohr soo-n*ooz*
Can I have a bag, please?	**Bir çanta veriniz, lütfen**
	beer ch*ah*n-tah veh-ree-n*eez* looht-fehn
Can I have a receipt?	**Bir makbuz veriniz**
	beer mahk-b*ooz* veh-ree-n*eez*
Do you take . . .	**. . . alır mısınız?**
	ah-l*uh*r muh-suh-n*uh*z
English/American money?	**İngiliz/Amerikan parası**
	een-ghee-l*eez*/ah-meh-ree-k*ah*n pah-rah-s*uh*
travellers' cheques?	**Seyahat çeki**
	seh-yah-h*ah*t cheh-k*ee*
credit cards?	**Kredi kartı**
	kreh-d*ee* kahr-t*uh*
I'd like . . .	**. . . istiyorum**
	ees-*tee*-yoh-room
one like that	**Bir tane bunun gibi**
	beer tah-neh boo-n*oon* gee-b*ee*
two like that	**İki tane bunun gibi**
	ee-kee tah-neh boo-n*oon* gee-b*ee*

SHOP ASSISTANT

Can I help you?	**Size yardım edebilir miyim?**
	see-zeh yahr-duhm eh-deh-bee-leer
	mee-yeem
What would you like?	**Ne istersiniz?**
	neh ees-tehr-see-neez
Will that be all?	**Başka bir şey var mı?**
	bahsh-kah beer shehy vahr muh
Would you like anything else?	**Başka bir şey ister misiniz?**
	bahsh-kah beer shehy ees-tehr
	mee-see-neez
Would you like it wrapped?	**Paket yapılım mı?**
	pah-keht yah-puh-luhm muh
Sorry, none left	**Özür dilerim, kalmadı**
	er-zoohr dee-leh-reem kahl-mah-
	duh
I haven't got any	**Yok**
	yohk
How many do you want?	**Kaç tane istersiniz?**
	kahch tah-neh ees-tehr-see-neez
Is that enough?	**Bu kadar yeter mi?**
	boo kah-dahr yeh-tehr mee

Shopping for food

Bread

ESSENTIAL INFORMATION

● For finding a baker's, see p. 17.
● Key words to look for:
  EKMEK (bread)
  EKMEKÇİ (baker)
  FIRIN (bakery)

- Bread is the staple food in Turkey and there are numerous bakeries everywhere. They open early in the morning and stay open till late at night. Supermarket, delicatessens and grocery stores also sell bread.
- Bread is sold by weight, the standard loaf being 1 kg. However, one normally asks for a certain number of loaves rather than a certain weight. Note that 'ekmek' in Turkish means both 'bread' and 'loaf'. You can buy just half a loaf if you want only a small amount.

WHAT TO SAY

Some bread, please	**Ekmek, lütfen**
	ehk-mehk looht-fehn
One loaf (like that)	**Bir ekmek (şundan)**
	beer ehk-mehk (shoon-dahn)
A loaf	**Bir ekmek**
	beer ehk-mehk
Half a loaf	**Yarım ekmek**
	yah-ruhm ehk-mehk
A wholewheat loaf	**Bir kepek ekmeği**
	beer keh-pehk ehk-meh-*ee*
A French-style loaf	**Bir uzun ekmek**
	beer oo-zoon ehk-mehk
A 'milk' loaf [*made from dough to which milk is added*]	**Bir sütlü ekmek**
	beer sooht-looh ehk-mehk
A crescent-shaped loaf	**Bir ay**
	beer ay
A loaf of rye bread	**Bir çavdar ekmeği**
	beer chahv-dahr ehk-meh-*ee*
A bread roll	**Bir sandviç ekmeği**
	beer sahnd-veech ehk-meh-*ee*
Some sliced bread	**Tost ekmeği**
	tohst ehk-meh-*ee*
Two loaves	**İki ekmek**
	ee-kee ehk-mehk
Four bread rolls	**Dört sandviç ekmeği**
	derrt sahnd-veech ehk-meh-*ee*

[*For other essential expressions, see 'Shop talk', p. 50*]

Cakes, ice-cream and sweets

ESSENTIAL INFORMATION

- Key words to look out for:
  BÖREKÇİ (pastry shop)
  DONDURMA (ice-cream)
  KURUYEMİŞÇİ (dried fruit, nut and sweet shop)
  MUHALLEBECİ (chicken, pudding, sweet and ice-cream shop)
  PASTANE (pastry and cake shop)
  ŞEKERLEME (confectionery)
  ŞEKERÇİ (confectionery shop)
- To find a cake shop etc., see p. 17.
- To order a snack, see p. 76.
- A vast range of pastries, cakes, puddings and sweets is available in Turkey. The list at the end of this section contains a selection of some of the best known.

WHAT TO SAY

Pastries and sweets are sold by weight, but with small items and slices of cakes and pastries you can always ask for them by portion, i.e. enough for one person, two people, etc.

100 grams of . . .	**Yüz gram . . .** yoohz grahm
200 grams of . . .	**İki yüz gram . . .** ee-k*ee* yoohz grahm
½ kilo of . . .	**Yarım kilo . . .** yah-r*uh*m kee-l*oh*
1 portion of . . .	**Bir porsiyon** beer pohr-see-y*ohn*
2 portions of . . .	**İki porsiyon** ee-k*ee* pohr-see-y*ohn*
5 portions of . . .	**Beş porsiyon . . .** behsh pohr-see-y*ohn*
chocolate cake	**çikolatalı pasta** ch*ee*-koh-lah-tah-l*uh* p*a*hs-tah
apple tart	**elmalı torta** ehl-mah-l*uh* tohr-t*a*h

mixed fruit tart	**karışık torta**
	kah-ruh-shuhk tohr-tah
Turkish delight	**lokum**
	loh-koom
baklava [see list below]	**baklava**
	bahk-lah-vah

Some pastries come in two versions, one savoury, made with salt, the other sweet, made with sugar. So you might be given a choice of:

with salt	**tuzlu**
	tooz-loo
with sugar	**şekerli**
	sheh-kehr-lee

The word for ice-cream is **dondurma**.

I'd like a(n) . . . ice-cream	**Bir . . . dondurma istiyorum**
	beer . . . dohn-door-meh ees-tee-yoh-room
apricot	**kayısılı**
	kah-yuh-suh-luh
cherry	**vişneli**
	veesh-neh-lee
chocolate	**çikolatalı**
	chee-koh-lah-tah-luh
lemon	**limonlu**
	lee-mohn-loo
pistachio	**fıstıklı**
	fuhs-tuk-luh
strawberry	**çilekli**
	chee-lehk-lee
vanilla	**vanilyalı**
	vah-neel-yah-luh
An ice-cream with whipped cream	**Bir şantiyeli dondurma**
	beer shahn-tee-yeh-lee dohn-door-mah
A chocolate-coated ice on a stick	**Bir panda**
	beer pahn-dah
A packet of . . .	**Bir paket . . .**
	beer pah-keht

chocolates   **çikolata**
chee-koh-l*ah*-tah

pistachio nuts   **fıstık**
fuhs-t*u*hk

You may also like to try the following:

aşure
ah-sh*oo*-reh

pudding made from wheat, walnuts, raisins, figs etc.

baklava
bahk-lah-v*ah*

layered pastry stuffed with nuts and/or cream, steeped in syrup

badem kurabiyesi
bah-d*eh*m koo-rah-bee-yeh-s*ee*

almond cake

bülbül yuvası
boohl-b*oo*hl yoo-vah-s*u*h

'nightingale's nest': pastry in the shape of a nest, stuffed with walnuts

dilber dudağı
deel-b*eh*r doo-dah-*u*h

'beloved's lips': sponge and syrup pudding in the shape of lips

güllaç
goohl-l*ah*ch

layered pastry with almonds cooked in milk

hanım göbeği
hah-n*u*hm gher-beh-*ee*

'lady's navel': sponge with hole in the middle, steeped in syrup

hanım parmağı
hah-n*u*hm pahr-mah-*u*h

'lady's finger': sponge fingers in syrup

helva
hehl-v*ah*

halva: crumbly cake of chopped nuts, honey and sesame seeds

kabak tatlısı
kah-b*ah*k taht-luh-s*u*h

sweet pumpkin sprinkled with chopped walnuts

kadayıf
kah-dah-y*u*hf

shredded wheat with nuts and syrup

keşkül-ü fırkara
kehsh-k*oo*hl-ooh fuhr-kah-r*ah*

milk pudding with almonds or pistachios

lokma
lohk-m*ah*

doughnut in syrup

lokum
loh-k*oo*m

Turkish delight: comes in a variety of flavours, with or without nuts

muhallebi
moo-hahl-leh-b*ee*

milk pudding

pelte
pehl-t*eh*

jelly

sarığı burma
sah-ruh-*u*h boor-m*ah*

'twisted turban': baklava in shape of a turban

sütlaç	rice pudding
sooht-*lah*ch	
tavuk göğsü	blancmange-like milk pudding
tah-w*oo*k gher-s*oo*h	made with pounded chicken
	breast sprinkled with cinnamon
tulumba tatlısı	semolina doughsticks in syrup
too-loom-b*ah* taht-luh-s*uh*	
vezir parmağı	'vizier's finger': sponge finger in
veh-z*ee*r pahr-mah-*uh*	syrup
zerde	sweet rice with saffron
zehr-d*eh*	

In the supermarket

ESSENTIAL INFORMATION

- The signs to look out for are:
  ANKARA PAZARI ⎤
  MİGROS   ⎟ supermarket chains
  SÜPERMARKET ⎦
- Supermarkets are a relatively new phenomenon in Turkey and
  none of them is very large. However, they are gradually becoming
  more common in the larger cities and resorts. The words in this
  section should also be useful in ordinary grocery stores
  (**BAKKAL**).
- For non-food items, see 'Replacing equipment', p. 48.
- No need to say anything in a supermarket, but ask if you can't
  find what you want.

WHAT TO SAY

Excuse me, please	**Affedersiniz**
	ahf-feh-dehr-see-n*ee*z
Where is . . .	**. . . nerede?**
	neh-reh-d*eh*
the bread?	**Ekmek**
	ehk-m*eh*k

the butter?	**Tereyağı**
	teh-reh-yah-*uh*
the cheese?	**Peynir**
	pehy-n*ee*r
the chocolate?	**Çikolata**
	chee-koh-l*ah*-tah
the coffee?	**Kahve**
	kah-v*eh*
the cooking oil?	**Sıvı yağ**
	suh-v*uh* yah
the frozen food?	**Dondurulmuş yiyecekler**
	dohn-doo-rool-m*oo*sh yee-yeh-jehk-l*eh*r
the fruit?	**Meyva**
	mehy-v*ah*
the fruit juice?	**Meyva suyu**
	mehy-v*ah* soo-y*oo*
the jam?	**Reçel**
	reh-chehl
the meat?	**Et**
	eht
the milk?	**Süt**
	sooht
the mineral water?	**Maden suyu**
	mah-dehn soo-y*oo*
the pasta?	**Makarna**
	mah-k*ah*r-nah
the salt?	**Tuz**
	tooz
the sugar?	**Şeker**
	sheh-k*eh*r
the tea?	**Çay**
	chay
the tinned fish?	**Konserve balık**
	kohn-s*eh*r-veh bah-l*uh*k
the tinned fruit?	**Konserve meyva**
	kohn-s*eh*r-veh mehy-v*ah*
the vegetables?	**Sebze**
	sehb-z*eh*
the vinegar?	**Sirke**
	seer-k*eh*
the wine?	**Şarap**
	shah-r*ah*p

the yogurt?	**Yoğurt**
	yoh-*oo*rt
Where are . . .	**. . . nerede?**
	neh-reh-d*e*h
the biscuits?	**Bisküvitler**
	bee-skooh-veet-l*e*hr
crisps?	**Cips**
	jeeps
the eggs?	**Yumurta**
	yoo-moor-t*a*h
the seafoods?	**Deniz ürünleri**
	deh-n*ee*z ooh-roohn-leh-r*ee*
the soft drinks?	**Meşrubat**
	mehsh-roo-b*a*ht
the sweets?	**Tatlılar**
	taht-luh-l*a*hr
the tinned vegetables?	**Konserve sebze**
	kohn-sehr-veh sehb-z*e*h

[*For other essential expressions, see 'Shop talk', p. 50*]

Picnic food

ESSENTIAL INFORMATION

- Key words to look for:
  BAKKAL (grocer)
  ŞARKÜTERİ (delicatessen)
- Weight guide:
  4–6oz/150g of prepared salad per two people, if eaten as a starter to a substantial meal.
  3–4oz/100g of prepared salad per person, if to be eaten as the main part of a picnic-type meal.
- Since Turkey is predominantly a Muslim country, pork products are not easy to find.
- Chicken roasted on the spit can be bought to take away at many small restaurants. Look out for the sign **PAKET SERVİSİ** (take-away service).

WHAT TO SAY

One slice of . . .	**Bir dilim . . .**
	beer dee-l*ee*m
Two slices of . . .	**İki dilim . . .**
	ee-k*ee* dee-l*ee*m
roast beef	**rozbif**
	rohz-b*ee*f
tongue	**dil**
	d*ee*l
ham	**jambon**
	jahm-b*oh*n
garlic sausage	**sucuk**
	soo-j*oo*k
salami	**salam**
	sah-l*ah*m
100 grams of . . .	**Yüz gram . . .**
	yoohz grahm
150 grams of . . .	**Yüz elli gram . . .**
	yoohz ehl-l*ee* grahm
200 grams of . . .	**İki yüz gram . . .**
	ee-k*ee* yoohz grahm
300 grams of . . .	**Üç yüz gram . . .**
	oohch yoohz grahm
Russian salad	**Rus salatası**
	roos sah-lah-tah-s*u*h
tomato salad	**domates salatası**
	doh-m*ah*-tehs sah-lah-tah-s*u*h
beetroot salad	**pancar salatası**
	pahn-j*ah*r sah-lah-tah-s*u*h
carrot salad	**havuç salatası**
	hah-v*oo*ch sah-lah-tah-s*u*h
green salad	**yeşil salata**
	yeh-sh*ee*l sah-l*ah*-tah
olives	**zeytin**
	zehy-t*ee*n
anchovies	**ançüvez**
	ahn-ch*oo*h-vehz
cheese	**peynir**
	pehy-n*ee*r
A (pot of) mayonnaise	**Bir mayonez**
	beer mah-yoh-n*e*hz

A (pot of) mustard

Bir hardal
beer hahr-d*a*hl

You might also like to try some of these:

acılı
ah-juh-l*u*h

cracked wheat,* tomato, parsley
and hot pepper salad

cacık
jah-j*u*hk

yogurt and cucumber salad

haydari
hay-dah-r*ee*

cheese and yogurt dip

midye salatası
m*ee*d-yeh sah-lah-tah-s*u*h

mussel salad

pastırma
pahs-tuhr-m*a*h

pastrami, spiced dried beef

yaprak dolması
yah-pr*a*hk dohl-mah-s*u*h

stuffed vine leaves

These are the most commonly available cheeses:

beyaz peynir
beh-y*a*hz pehy-n*ee*r

white cheese, made from sheep's
milk, like Greek feta cheese

Çerkez peyniri
chehr-k*e*hz pehy-nee-r*ee*

a mild soft unsalted cheese

dil peyniri
deel pehy-nee-r*ee*

a mild cheddar-like cheese

gravyer
grahv-y*e*hr

a gruyère-type cheese

kaşer
kah-sh*e*hr

a cheddar-like cheese

tulum peyniri
too-l*oo*m pehy-nee-r*ee*

a hard salty cheese in a rind

*Also known as burghul or bulgur.

Fruit and vegetables

ESSENTIAL INFORMATION

- Key words to look for:
  MEYVA/MEYVE (fruit)
  SEBZELER (vegetables)
  MANAV (greengrocer)
- If possible, buy fruit and vegetables in the market, where they are cheaper than in the shops.
- A kilo is roughly equivalent to 2lbs.

WHAT TO SAY

½ kilo of . . .	**Yarım kilo . . .** yah-ruhm kee-loh
1 kilo of . . .	**Bir kilo . . .** beer kee-loh
2 kilos of . . .	**İki kilo . . .** ee-kee kee-loh
apples	**elma** ehl-mah
bananas	**muz** mooz
cherries	**kiraz** kee-rahz
grapes	**üzüm** ooh-zoohm
oranges	**portakal** pohr-tah-kahl
pears	**armut** ahr-moot
peaches	**şeftali** shehf-tah-lee
plums	**erik** eh-reek
strawberries	**çilek** chee-lehk
A pineapple, please	**Bir ananas, lütfen** beer ah-nah-nahs looht-fehn

A grapefruit	**Bir greyfrut**
	beer grehy-fr*oo*t
A melon	**Bir kavun**
	beer kah-w*oo*n
A water melon	**Bir karpuz**
	beer kahr-p*oo*z
1 kilo of . . .	**Bir kilo . . .**
	beer kee-l*oh*
artichokes	**enginar**
	ehn-ghee-n*a*hr
aubergines	**patlıcan**
	paht-luh-j*a*hn
carrots	**havuç**
	hah-w*oo*ch
courgettes	**kabak**
	kah-b*a*hk
green beans	**yeşil fasulye**
	yeh-sh*ee*l fah-s*oo*l-yeh
leeks	**pırasa**
	puh-r*a*h-sah
mushrooms	**mantar**
	mahn-t*a*hr
onions	**soğan**
	soh-*a*hn
peas	**bezelye**
	beh-zehl-y*e*h
potatoes	**patates**
	pah-t*a*h-tehs
red cabbage	**kırmızı lahana**
	kuhr-muh-z*u*h lah-hah-nah
spinach	**ıspanak**
	uhs-pah-n*a*hk
tomatoes	**domates**
	doh-m*a*h-tes
A bunch of parsley	**Bir demet maydanoz**
	beer deh-m*e*ht may-dah-n*o*hz
A bunch of radishes	**Bir demet turp**
	beer deh-m*e*ht toorp
A head of garlic	**Bir baş sarmısak**
	beer bahsh sahr-muh-s*a*hk
A lettuce	**Bir salata**
	beer sah-l*a*h-tah

A cauliflower   **Bir karnabahar**
beer kahr-nah-bah-h*a*r

A cabbage   **Bir lahana**
beer l*a*h-hah-nah

A cucumber   **Bir salatalık**
beer sah-lah-tah-l*u*hk

Like that, please   **Bundan, lütfen**
boon-d*a*hn l*oo*ht-fehn

You might also like to try these:

kabak	pumpkin
kah-b*a*hk	
kereviz	celery root
keh-reh-v*ee*z	
nar	pomegranate
nahr	
ayva	quince
ay-v*a*h	

[*For other essential information, see 'Shop talk', p. 50*]

Meat

ESSENTIAL INFORMATION

- Key words to look out for:
  KASAP (butcher)
  CİĞERCİ (offal shop)
- Weight guide: 4–6oz/125–200g of meat per person for one meal.
- A wide range of cuts is available, though you may not find exactly the same ones as at home. If in doubt, tell the butcher whether you intend to stew, grill or roast the meat, so that he will know what to give you.
- Offal is very popular in Turkey and a full range is available in special shops called **CİĞERCİ**.
- If you want the best-quality mince, choose a piece of meat and ask the butcher to mince it for you.

- Mutton tends to have a stronger flavour than most English palates are nowadays accustomed to.
- Turkey is predominantly a Muslim country, so pork (**domuz**) is very difficult to find.

WHAT TO SAY

For a joint, choose the type of meat you want and then say how many people it is for and how you intend to cook it.

Some beef, please	**Sığır, lütfen** suh-*u*hr l*oo*ht-fehn
Some lamb	**Kuzu** koo-z*oo*
Some mutton	**Koyun** koh-y*oo*n
Some veal	**Dana** dah-n*a*h
A joint . . .	**Rostoluk et . . .** rohs-toh-l*oo*k eht
Meat for shish kebabs . . .	**Şişlik et . . .** sheesh-l*ee*k eht
for two people	**iki kişi için** ee-k*ee* kee-sh*ee* ee-cheen
for four people	**dört kişi için** derrt kee-sh*ee* ee-cheen
for six people	**altı kişi için** ahl-t*u*h kee-sh*ee* ee-cheen
I want . . . the meat	**Eti . . . istiyorum** eh-t*ee* . . . ees-t*ee*-yoh-room
to boil	**haşlamalık** hahsh-lah-mah-l*u*hk
to grill	**ızgaralık** uhz-gah-rah-l*u*hk
to roast	**kavurmalık** kah-voor-mah-l*u*hk

For steak, liver or kidneys, do as above.

Some steak, please	**Biftek, lütfen** beef-t*e*hk l*oo*ht-fehn

Sirloin steak	**Bonfile** bohn-fee-leh
Some liver	**Ciğer** jee-ehr
Some kidneys	**Böbrek** ber-brehk
for three people	**üç kişi için** oohch kee-shee ee-cheen
for five people	**beş kişi için** behsh kee-shee ee-cheen

For chops, do it this way:

Two veal escalopes, please	**İki dana eskalop, lütfen** ee-kee dah-nah ehs-kah-lohp looht-fehn
Five lamb chops	**Beş kuzu pirzolası** behsh koo-zoo peer-zoh-lah-suh

Beef and veal
Sığır ve dana

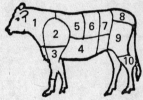

1 Gerdan
2 Kürek
3 Kol
4 Göğüs; döş
5 Pirzola
6 File
7 Antrekotlet
8 Sokum
9 Tranş; nua
10 Bacak

Lamb and mutton
Kuzu ve koyun

1 Kol
2 Kürek
3 Pirzola
4 Fileto
5 Göğüs
6 But

You may also want:

A chicken	**Piliç**
	pee-*lee*ch
A duck	**Ördek**
	err-d*e*hk
Quail	**Bıldırcın**
	buhl-duhr-j*u*hn
A rabbit	**Tavşan**
	tahv-sh*a*hn
Some tongue	**Dil**
	deel

Other essential expressions (*see also p. 50*):

Please . . .	**Lütfen . . .**
	l*oo*ht-fehn
mince it	**kıyınız**
	kuh-yuh-n*u*hz
dice it	**kuşbaşı**
	koosh-bah-sh*u*h
trim the fat	**yağını çıkartınız**
	yah-uh-n*u*h chuh-kahr-tuh-n*u*hz

Fish

ESSENTIAL INFORMATION

- Look out for:
  BALIKÇI (fishmonger)
- Fish can also be bought in fish markets and, in ports, on the quay where the fishing boats come in.

- Weight guide: 8oz/250g minimum per person for one meal of fish bought on the bone.
  i.e. ½ kilo/500g   for two people
  1 kilo   for four people
  1½ kilo   for six people
- It is not normal practice in Turkey for the fishmonger to fillet fish, and you may also find that some fishmongers will not clean fish – so bear this in mind when choosing what to buy.
- A wide range of excellent fresh fish is available in the coastal regions, according of course to season. Some types of fish will be unfamiliar but well worth trying, as many are delicious.

WHAT TO SAY

Fish is bought by the kilo or, with larger fish and some shellfish, it can also be bought by the item ('**tane**' in Turkish).
[*For numbers, see p. 118*]

½ kilo of	**Yarım kilo . . .**
	yah-r*u*hm kee-l*oh*
1 kilo of . . .	**Bir kilo . . .**
	beer kee-l*oh*
1½ kilo of . . .	**Bir buçuk kilo . . .**
	beer boo-ch*oo*k kee-l*oh*
One . . .	**Bir tane . . .**
	beer tah-n*eh*
Two . . .	**İki tane . . .**
	ee-k*ee* tah-n*eh*
Three . . .	**Üç tane . . .**
	oohch tah-n*eh*
anchovy	**hamsi**
	hahm-s*ee*
bass	**levrek**
	lehv-r*eh*k
blue fish	**lüfer**
	looh-f*eh*r
bonito	**palamut**
	pah-lah-m*oo*t
bream	**karagöz**
	kah-rah-g*er*z
brill	**pisi**
	pee-s*ee*

cod	**bakalyaro/mezgit**
	bah-kahl-yah-roh/mehz-geet
eel	**yılan balığı**
	yuh-lahn bah-luh-uh
gar fish	**zargana**
	zahr-gah-nah
gilt-head bream	**çipura**
	chee-poo-rah
goby	**kaya balığı**
	kah-yah bah-luh-uh
mackerel	**uskumru/kolyoz/istavrit**
	oos-koom-roo/kohl-yohz/ees-tah-vreet
mullet (grey)	**kefal**
	keh-fahl
mullet (red, small)	**tekir**
	teh-keer
mullet (red)	**barbunya**
	bahr-boon-yah
octopus	**ahtapod**
	ah-tah-pohd
pandora	**mercan**
	mehr-jahn
sandsmelt	**gümüş**
	gooh-moohsh
sardine	**sardalya**
	sahr-dahl-yah
scorpion fish	**iskorpit**
	ees-kohr-peet
squid	**kalamar**
	kah-lah-mahr
sole	**dil**
	deel
sturgeon	**mersin balığı**
	mehr-seen bah-luh-uh
swordfish	**kılıç balığı**
	kuh-luhch bah-luh-uh
tub fish	**kırlangıç balığı**
	kuhr-lahn-guhch bah-luh-uh
turbot	**kalkan**
	kahl-kahn
whiting	**mezgit/bakalyaro**
	mehz-geet/bah-kahl-yah-roh

Some large fish can be purchased by the slice:

One slice of . . .	**Bir dilim . . .**
	beer dee-*leem*
Two slices of . . .	**İki dilim . . .**
	ee-*kee* dee-*leem*
Six slices of . . .	**Altı dilim . . .**
	ahl-*tuh* dee-*leem*
cod	**bakalyaro**
	bah-kahl-*yah*-roh
tuna	**ton**
	tohn
turbot	**kalkan**
	kahl-*kahn*

Shellfish

Crab	**Yengeç/pavurya**
	yehn-*ghehch*/pah-*voor*-yah
Mussels	**Midye**
	m*eed*-yeh
Oysters	**İstiridye**
	ees-tee-*reed*-yeh
Prawns	**Karides**
	kah-*ree*-dehs
Scallops	**Tarak**
	tah-*rahk*
Shrimp	**Kerevet**
	keh-reh-*veht*

Other essential expressions (*see also p. 50*):

Please . . .	**Lütfen . . .**
	*loo*ht-fehn
take the head off	**kafayı çıkartınız**
	kah-fah-*yuh* chuh-kahr-tuh-*nuhz*
clean them	**temizleyiniz**
	teh-meez-leh-yee-*neez*

Eating and drinking out

Ordering a drink

ESSENTIAL INFORMATION

- Key words to look for:
  BAR
  BİRHANE (beer hall/pub)
  BÜFE (snack bar)
  ÇAYHANE (tea house)
  KAFETERİA (cafeteria)
  MEYHANE (tavern)
- Except in places where drinks are consumed standing at a counter, there is nearly always waiter service and one should leave a tip.
- Excellent fruit juices made from freshly pressed fruit are very popular in Turkey. Look for the sign **MEYVA SUYU** (fruit juice).
- Tea is the national hot drink in Turkey. It is served, without milk, in small glasses. During the summer there are many pleasant tea gardens (**ÇAY BAHÇESİ**) where people go to relax with their families and friends.
- The national alcoholic drink is **rakı**. This aniseed-flavoured grape spirit, which closely resembles Middle Eastern arak and Greek ouzo, is usually mixed with water and/or ice. **Rakı** is drunk both on its own and as an accompaniment to food.
- There are also locally produced gin and vodka, which are very much cheaper than imported brands, and a variety of Turkish wines, some of which are very drinkable.
- Bottled beer of the lager type is good quality and widely available. Some pubs and taverns serve draft lager – look out for the sign **FIÇI BİRA** (barrel beer).
- The **kahve**, or old-style Turkish coffee house, is an exclusively male preserve where the men go to talk, do business and play cards and backgammon. Tea and coffee, but not alcoholic drinks, are served.
- When asking for Turkish coffee, one specifies how sweet one wants it (because the sugar is added while the water and coffee nixture is being heated).

WHAT TO SAY

I'd like . . .	. . . **istiyorum**
	ees-*tee*-yoh-room
a Turkish coffee	**bir Türk kahvesi**
	beer toohrk kah-veh-s*ee*
without sugar	**Sade**
	s*a*h-deh
with a little sugar	**Az şekerli**
	ahz sheh-kehr-l*ee*
medium sweet	**Orta şekerli**
	ohr-t*a*h sheh-kehr-l*ee*
sweet	**Şekerli**
	sheh-kehr-l*ee*
a (black) coffee	**bir neskafé**
	beer nehs-kah-feh
with milk	**Sütlü**
	sooht-l*oo*h
a tea	**bir çay**
	beer ch*a*y
with milk	**Sütlü**
	sooht-l*oo*h
with lemon	**Limonlu**
	lee-mohn-l*oo*
a glass of milk	**Bir süt**
	beer sooht
two glasses of milk	**İki süt**
	ee-k*ee* sooht
a drinking chocolate	**Bir sütlü kakao**
	beer sooht-l*oo*h kah-kah-*oh*
a mineral water	**Bir maden suyu**
	beer mah-d*e*hn soo-y*oo*
a lemonade	**Bir limonata**
	beer lee-moh-n*a*h-tah
a lemon juice	**Bir limon suyu**
	beer lee-m*o*hn soo-y*oo*
a Coca Cola	**Bir Koka Kola**
	beer k*o*h-kah k*o*h-lah
an orangeade	**Bir portakallı gazoz**
	beer pohr-tah-kahl-l*u*h gah-z*o*hz
an orange juice	**Bir portakal suyu**
	beer pohr-tah-k*a*hl soo-y*oo*

a grape juice	**Bir üzüm suyu**
	beer ooh-z*oo*hm soo-y*oo*
a pineapple juice	**Bir ananas suyu**
	beer ah-nah-n*a*hs soo-y*oo*
a small bottle of beer	**Küçük bir bira**
	kooh-ch*oo*hk beer b*ee*-rah
a large bottle of beer	**Büyük bir bira**
	booh-y*oo*hk beer b*ee*-rah
a draught beer	**bir fıçı birası**
	beer fuh-ch*u*h bee-rah-s*u*h
small	**Kücük**
	kooh-ch*oo*k
large	**Büyük**
	booh-y*oo*hk
a bottle of wine	**Bir şişe şarap**
	beer shee-sheh shah-r*a*hp
a small bottle of wine	**Küçük bir şişe şarap**
	kooh-ch*oo*hk beer shee-sheh shah-r*a*hp
red	**kırmızı**
	kuhr-muh-z*u*h
white	**beyaz**
	beh-y*a*hz
rosé	**roze**
	roh-z*e*h
dry	**sek**
	sehk
medium sweet	**demi sek**
	deh-m*ee* sehk
sparkling	**köpüklü**
	ker-poohk-l*oo*
A bottle of champagne	**Bir şişe şampanya**
	beer shee-sheh shahm-p*a*hn-yah
A whisky	**Bir viski**
	beer v*ee*s-kee
with ice	**buz ile**
	booz ee-l*e*h
with (mineral) water	**(maden) suyu ile**
	(mah-d*e*hn) soo-y*oo* ee-l*e*h
with soda	**soda ile**
	s*o*h-dah ee-l*e*h

A gin	**Bir cin** beer jeen
A gin and tonic	**Bir cin-tonik** beer jeen-toh-neek
with lemon	**limon ile** lee-mohn ee-leh
A vodka	**Bir votka** beer voht-kah
A vodka and tonic	**Bir votka-tonik** beer voht-kah-toh-neek
A brandy	**Bir konyak** beer kohn-yahk

You may also like to try these local beverages:

ayran ay-rahn	a yogurt drink (very slightly salty) served cold; very popular, especially in summer
boza boh-zah	a winter drink made from fermented millet sprinkled with cinnamon
salep sah-lehp	another winter drink made of hot milk flavoured with orchis root and sprinkled with cinnamon

Other essential expressions:

Waiter!	**Bakar mısınız!** bah-kahr muh-suh-nuhz
The bill, please	**Hesabı, lütfen** heh-sah-buh looht-fehn
How much?	**Ne kadar?** neh kah-dahr
Is service included?	**Servis dahil mi?** sehr-vees dah-heel mee
Where is the toilet, please?	**Tuvalet nerede, lütfen?** too-wah-leht neh-reh-deh looht-fehn

Ordering a snack

ESSENTIAL INFORMATION

- Look out for these signs:
  BAR
  BÖREKÇİ (pastry shop)
  BÜFE (snack bar)
  CAFE
  KAFETERİA (cafeteria)
- All the above places serve drinks as well as food (though some places serve only soft drinks).
- Look for the names of snacks in the windows.
- For cakes, ice-creams and sweets, see p. 55.
- For picnic-type snacks, see p. 60.
- Note that in Turkey a '**sandviç**' means a roll with a filling, rather than a 'sandwich'. However, toasted sandwiches – '**tost**' – are made with sliced bread.

WHAT TO SAY

I'd like . . .	. . . istiyorum
	ees-*tee*-yoh-room
a cheese roll	**Bir peynirli sandviç**
	beer pehy-neer-*lee* sahnd-v*ee*ch
an egg roll	**Bir yumurtalı sandviç**
	beer yoo-moor-tah-l*uh* sahnd-v*ee*ch
a hamburger	**Bir hamburger**
	beer hahm-boor-gh*e*hr
a hot dog	**Bir sosisli sandviç**
	beer soh-sees-*lee* sahnd-v*ee*ch
a toasted sandwich	**Bir tost**
	beer tohst
an ice-cream	**Bir dondurma**
	beer dohn-door-m*a*h
a bag of crisps	**Bir paket cips**
	beer pah-k*e*ht jeeps

You may also like to try the following:

börek ber-*rehk*	savoury pastries filled with cheese, minced meat, spinach etc.
lâhmacun lah-mah-*joon*	Turkish-style pizza: soft bread topped with minced meat, chopped tomatoes and red pepper, served hot
leblebi lehb-leh-*bee*	roasted chickpeas, prepared in various ways, salted and unsalted, sold either by dried fruit shops (**KURUYEMİŞÇİ**) or street vendors
midye tava m*ee*d-yeh tah-v*ah*	mussels on sticks, deep-fried in batter, available from street vendors
simit see-m*ee*t	bread rings covered in sesame seeds, sold by street vendors

[*For other essential expressions, see 'Ordering a drink', p. 72*]

In a restaurant

ESSENTIAL INFORMATION

- The place to ask for: **bir lokanta**
- You can eat at these places:
  BALIK LOKANTASI (fish restaurant)
  BÖREKÇİ (for savoury pastries)
  İSKEMBECİ (restaurant specializing in tripe soup)
  KEBABÇİ (kebab restaurant)
  KÖFTECİ (for grilled Turkish-style hamburger)
  LOKANTA (restaurant)
  MUHALLEBİCİ (restaurant specializing in chicken)
  PİDECİ (for Turkish-style pizzas)
  RESTORAN (restaurant)
- By law menus and prices must be displayed in the restaurant.

- In self-service restaurants you choose what you want from a display of hot and cold dishes and then, usually, your tray is brought by a waiter to your table.
- A service charge of 10% is generally included in the bill. However, it is customary to leave a further tip of about 5–10% (or even more – if you are pleased with the service).
- Eating times tend to be earlier than in other Mediterranean countries.
- Not all restaurants serve alcoholic drinks, so if you do want a drink with your meal check before you order.

WHAT TO SAY

May I book a table?	**Rezervasyon yapabilir miyim?** reh-zehr-vahs-yohn yah-pah-bee-leer mee-yeem
I've booked a table	**Rezervasyonum var** reh-zehr-vahs-yoh-noom vahr
A table . . .	**. . . masa** mah-sah
for one	**Bir kişilik** beer kee-shee-leek
for three	**Üç kişilik** oohch kee-shee-leek
The menu, please	**Mönüyü, lütfen** mer-nooh-yooh looht-fehn
The fixed-price menu	**Tabldot** tahbl-doh
The tourist menu	**Turistik mönüyü** too-rees-teek mer-nooh-yooh
Today's special menu	**Bugünkü mönüyü** boo-goohn-kooh mer-nooh-yooh
What's this, please?	**Bu ne, lütfen?** boo neh looht-fehn
Some wine, please	**Şarap, lütfen** shah-rahp looht-fehn
A bottle	**Bir şişe** beer shee-sheh
A half-bottle	**Yarım şişe** yah-ruhm shee-sheh
Red/white/rosé	**Kırmızı/beyaz/roze** kuhr-muh-zuh/beh-yahz/roh-zeh

Some beer	**Bira**
	b*ee*-rah
Some more bread, please	**Biraz daha ekmek, lütfen**
	bee-r*a*hz dah-h*a*h ehk-m*e*hk looht-
	fehn
Some more wine	**Daha şarap**
	dah-h*a*h shah-r*a*hp
Some oil	**Yağı**
	yah-*u*h
Some vinegar	**Sirke**
	seer-k*e*h
Some salt	**Tuz**
	tooz
Some pepper	**Biber**
	bee-b*e*hr
Some mineral water	**Maden suyu**
	mah-d*e*hn soo-y*oo*
How much does that come to?	**Borçum ne kadar?**
	bohr-ch*oo*m neh kah-d*a*hr
Is service included?	**Servis dahil mi?**
	sehr-v*ee*s dah-h*ee*l mee
Where is the toilet, please?	**Tuvalet nerede, lütfen?**
	too-wah-l*e*ht neh-reh-d*e*h looht-
	fehn
Excuse me! [*when trying to get the waiter's attention*]	**Bakar mısınız!**
	bah-k*a*hr muh-suh-n*u*hz
The bill, please	**Hesabı, lütfen**
	heh-sah-b*u*h looht-fehn
May I have a receipt	**Bir makbuz veriniz**
	beer mahk-b*oo*z veh-ree-n*ee*z

Key words for courses as seen on some menus

[*Only ask this question if you want the waiter to remind you of the choice*]

What have you got in the way of . . .	**. . . olarak ne var?**
	oh-lah-r*a*hk neh vahr
STARTERS?	**MEZE**
	meh-z*e*h
SOUP?	**ÇORBA**
	chohr-b*a*h

EGG DISHES?	**YUMURTA**
	yoo-moor-*tah*
FISH?	**BALIK**
	bah-*luh*k
MEAT?	**ET**
	eht
MAIN DISHES?	**ANA YEMEK**
	ah-*nah* yeh-m*eh*k
GRILLS?	**IZGARA**
	uhz-gah-r*ah*
VEGETABLES?	**SEBZE**
	sehb-z*eh*
SALADS?	**SALATA**
	sah-*lah*-tah
CHEESE?	**PEYNİR**
	pehy-n*eer*
FRUIT?	**MEYVA**
	mehy-v*ah*
ICE-CREAM?	**DONDURMA**
	dohn-door-m*ah*
DESSERTS?	**TATLI**
	taht-l*uh*

UNDERSTANDING THE MENU

- You will find that some menus in Turkey are in one or more European languages. However, if in doubt ask to look at the different dishes – the staff will always be happy to show you.
- It is the custom in many places to bring a large tray of starters (**mezeler**) to the table from which you can choose the ones you want.
- If something is brought to the table that you do not want, do not hesitate to say so – it will not cause offence.
- You will find the names of the principal ingredients of most dishes on these pages:

Starters, see p. 62   Fruit, see p. 63
Meat, see p. 65   Dessert, see p. 57
Fish, see p. 68   Cheese, see p. 62
Vegetables, see p. 63   Ice-cream, see p. 55

- The following list of cooking and menu terms should help you to decode the menu.

Cooking and menu terms

Adana kebabı	hot, spicy minced meat kebab
acılı	salad of cracked wheat, tomato and chopped hot red peppers
ançüvez	anchovies
Arnavut ciğeri	'Albanian liver': spicy diced liver served with raw onions
ayva	quince
az pişmiş	rare
balık	fish
balık çorbası	fish soup
balık köftesi	fried fish cakes
bamya	okra, ladies' fingers
beyin ızgara	grilled lamb's brains
beyin salatası	lamb's brains with oil and lemon juice
bezelye	peas
beyaz peynir	white sheep's milk cheese, like Greek feta
biber dolması	stuffed green pepper
biftek	steak
bonfile	sirloin steak
böbrek ızgara	grilled kidneys
börek	pastry with various savoury fillings, baked or deep fried
buğulama	steamed, poached
bulgur	cracked wheat
Bursa kebabı	grilled lamb with pitta bread, tomato and yoghurt
cacık	yoghurt with chopped cucumber and garlic
ciğer	liver
Çerkez tavuğu	'Circassian chicken': chicken served with walnut and garlic sauce
çevirme	roasted on a spit
çiğ	raw
Çoban salatası	'shepherd's salad': chopped tomato, cucumber, green pepper, parsley and onions
çok pişmiş	well done

çorba	soup
çömlek kebabı	meat and vegetable stew
deniz ürünleri	seafood
dil	tongue, or sole
dil söğüş	cold sliced tongue
dolma	stuffed vegetables
domates	tomato
domates salatası	tomato salad
döner kebap	slices of grilled lamb cut from meat cooked on a vertical spit
düğün çorbası	'wedding soup': lamb broth cooked with eggs and lemon
ekmek	bread
enginar	artichokes
et	meat
etli	with meat
ezme	purée
fasulye	beans
fasulye pilâki	cold beans in olive oil
fasulye piyazi	beans and onions
fava	puréed beans
fırında	baked or roasted in the oven
günün çorbası	soup of the day
güveç	meat and vegetable casserole
hamsi	anchovies
haşlama	boiled, stewed
kaynamış yumurta	boiled egg
havuç	carrots
haydari	white cheese mashed in yoghurt with thyme
hıyar	cucumber
hünkar beğendi	'emperor's delight': roast lamb with puréed aubergine
ıspanak	spinach
ıspanaklı börek	pastry with a spinach filling
ızgara	grilled
iç pilav	rice with chopped liver and pine nuts
içki	alcoholic drink
içli köfte	spiced minced meat, fried in a cracked wheat casing

imam bayıldı	'the imam fainted': aubergine stuffed with onion and tomato, cooked in olive oil and served cold
İskender kebap	a mixture of different kinds of kebab meat (**döner, şiş** etc.)
islim kebabı	lamb and vegetable pie
işkembe çorbası	tripe soup
iyi pişmiş	well-done
kabak	courgettes, marrow, pumpkin
kabak dolması	stuffed courgettes (zucchini)
kadın budu köfte	'lady's thigh': fried meatballs
kağıt kebabı	lamb and vegetables baked in paper
kağıtta pişmiş	baked in paper
kalamar	squid
kara zeytin	black olives
karides güveç	prawn casserole, with tomatoes and cheese
karnabahar	cauliflower
karnıyarık	aubergine with meat filling
kereviz	celery root
kısır	cracked wheat with paprika
kıymalı	with minced meat
kıymalı börek	pastry with mincemeat filling
kıvırcık salata	curly-leaved lettuce
kızartma	fried
koç yumurtası	'ram's eggs': ram's testicles
kotlet	cutlet
koyun eti	mutton
köfte	meatball, hamburger
kuru fasulye	green beans with tomato sauce
kuzu dolması	roast lamb with rice
kuzu eti	lamb
kuzu fırında	roast lamb
kuzu pirzolası	lamb chops
lahana dolması	stuffed cabbage leaves
lakerda salatası	sliced salted bonito (fish) salad
limon	lemon
Macar gulaşı	Hungarian goulash
maden suyu	mineral water
makarna	macaroni, pasta
mantar	mushrooms

mantı	Turkish-style ravioli
marul	lettuce
maydanoz	parsley
menemen	tomato and pepper omelette
mercimek	lentils
meşrubat	soft drinks
mevsim salatası	salad of the season
meze	starter, hors-d'oeuvre
midye dolması	mussels in their shells stuffed with rice and pine nuts
midye tava	mussels deep-fried on a stick in batter
muska böreği	triangles of pastry with various different fillings
omlet	omelette
Orman kebap	lamb casserole with carrots, potatoes and tomatoes
orta pişmiş	medium (cooked)
ördek	duck
paça	sheep's trotters in sauce
pancar	beetroot
pane	with breadcrumbs
pastırma	dried cured beef, pastrami
patates/tava kızartması	chips, french fries
patlıcan	aubergine
patlıcan dolması	stuffed aubergine
patlıcan salatası	aubergine salad
peynirli	with cheese
pilâki	white kidney beans in olive oil
pilav	rice
piliç	chicken
piliç ızgarası	grilled chicken
pirzola	a chop
pişkin	well-done
piyaz	green bean salad
roka	rocket, green salad leaf
rosto	roasted
Rus salatası	Russian salad
sahanda yumurta	fried eggs
salatalık	cucumber
salçalı	with tomato sauce
salçalı köfte	meatballs in tomato sauce
sandviç ekmek	bread roll

sarmısak	garlic
sebze çorbası	vegetable soup
sıcak	hot
sığır eti	beef
sigara böreği	pastry rolled into a cigarette shape with cheese or minced meat filling
soğan	onion
soğuk	cold
sosis	frankfurter-type sausage
soslu	with sauce
su böreği	baked layers of pastry stuffed with cheese or meat
sucuk	Turkish garlic sausage
şehriye	vermicelli
şiş kebap	skewered pieces of charcoal-grilled lamb
şiş köfte	skewered ground lamb meatballs, grilled
tarama salatası	smoked cod's roe salad
tas kebap	stewed meat in tomato sauce
tava	fried
tavuk	chicken
tavuk çorbası	chicken soup
terbiyeli	with egg and lemon sauce
tereyağı	butter
turp	radish
turşu	pickled vegetables
tükenmez	fried eggs with tomato and peppers
türlü	meat and vegetable stew
uykuluk	sweetbreads
viyana şinitzel	Wiener schnitzel
yahni	meat stewed with onions
yaprak dolması	stuffed vine or cabbage leaves
yaprak sarması	stuffed vine or cabbage leaves
yayla çorbası	yoghurt soup
yeşil salata	green salad
yeşil zeytin	green olives
yoğurtlu	with yoghurt
yumurta	egg
yumurtalı	with egg
yürek ızgara	grilled heart
zeytin	olives
zeytinyağlı	with olive oil

Health

ESSENTIAL INFORMATION

- In Turkey there are both State and privately run medical services. Turkish nationals receive free treatment in State hospitals, but many people with the funds to do so opt for the private system. When visiting Turkey it is essential to have proper medical insurance. A policy can be bought through a travel agent, a broker or a motoring organization.
- Take your own 'first line' first aid kit with you.
- For minor disorders and treatment at a chemist's, see p. 37.
- For finding your way to a doctor, dentist and chemist, see p. 17.
- Once in Turkey, decide on a definite plan of action in case of serious illness: communicate your problem to a near neighbour, the receptionist or someone you see regularly. You are then dependent on that person helping you obtain treatment.
- In an emergency, say **'Doktor istiyorum'** (dohk-tohr ees-tee-yoh-room): 'I need a doctor' – and if necessary keep saying **'Doktor'** until you get some response.
- Also look out for these signs:
  AMBULANS (ambulance)
  DİŞÇİ (dentist)
  GÖZLÜKÇÜ (optician)
  HASTANE (hospital)
  İLKYARDIM HASTANESİ (first aid hospital)
  KLİNİK (clinic)
  MUAYENEHANE (surgery)

WHAT'S THE MATTER

I have a pain . . .	. . . ağrıyor
	ah-ruh-yohr
in my abdomen	**Karnım**
	kahr-nuhm
in my ankle	**Ayak bileğim**
	ah-yahk bee-leh-eem
in my arm	**Kolum**
	koh-loom
in my back	**Sırtım**
	suhr-tuhm

in my bladder	**Mesânem**
	meh-sah-n*e*hm
in my bowels	**Barsaklarım**
	bahr-sahk-lah-r*u*hm
in my breast	**Göğsüm**
	gher-s*óo*hm
in my chest	**Göğsüm**
	gher-s*oo*hm
in my ear	**Kulağım**
	koo-lah-*u*hm
in my eye	**Gözüm**
	gher-z*oo*hm
in my foot	**Ayağım**
	ah-yah-*u*hm
in my head	**Başım**
	bah-sh*u*hm
in my heel	**Topuğum**
	toh-poo-*oo*m
in my jaw	**Çene kemiğim**
	cheh-n*e*h keh-mee-*ee*m
in my kidneys	**Böbreğim**
	ber-breh-*ee*m
in my leg	**Bacağım**
	bah-jah-*u*hm
in my lung	**Akciğerim**
	ahk-jee-eh-r*ee*m
in my neck	**Boynum**
	boy-n*oo*m
in my penis	**Penisim**
	peh-nee-s*ee*m
in my shoulder	**Omuzum**
	oh-moo-z*oo*m
in my stomach	**Midem**
	mee-d*e*hm
in my testicles	**Erbezlerim**
	ehr-behz-leh-r*ee*m
in my throat	**Boğazım**
	boh-ah-z*u*hm
in my vagina	**Vaginam**
	vah-ghee-n*a*hm
in my wrist	**Bileğim**
	bee-leh-*ee*m

I have a pain here [*point*]	**Buramda bir ağrı var**
	boo-rahm-d*a*h beer ah-r*u*h vahr
I have a toothache	**Dişim ağrıyor**
	dee-sh*ee*m ah-r*u*h-yohr
I have broken . . .	**. . . kırıldı**
	kuh-ruhl-d*u*h
my dentures	**Takma dişim**
	tahk-m*a*h dee-sh*ee*m
my glasses	**Gözlüğüm**
	gherz-looh-*oo*hm
I have lost my contact lens	**Kontakt lensimi kaybettim**
	kohn-t*a*hkt lehn-see-m*ee* kay-beht-teem
I have lost a filling	**Dolgum düştü**
	dohl-g*u*hm doohsh-t*oo*h
My child is ill	**Çocuğum hasta**
	choh-joo-*oo*m hahs-t*a*h
He/she has a pain here [*point*]	**Burası ağrıyor**
	boo-rah-suh ah-r*u*h-yohr

[*For parts of the body, see list above.*]

How bad is it?

I'm ill	**Hastayım**
	hah-stah-y*u*hm
It's urgent	**Acele**
	ah-jeh-l*e*h
It's serious	**Ağır**
	ah-*u*hr
It's not serious	**Önemi yok**
	er-neh-m*ee* yohk
It hurts	**Ağrıyor**
	ah-r*u*h-yohr
It hurts a lot	**Çok ağrıyor**
	chohk ah-r*u*h-yohr
It doesn't hurt much	**Çok ağrımıyor**
	chohk ah-r*u*h-muh-yohr
The pain occurs . . .	**Ağrısı tutuyor . . .**
	ah-ruh-s*u*h too-t*oo*-yohr
every quarter of an hour	**her çeyrek**
	hehr chehy-r*e*hk
every half-hour	**her yarım saat**
	hehr yah-r*u*hm sah-*a*ht

every hour	**her saat**
	hehr sah-*aht*
every day	**her gün**
	hehr goohn
most of the time	**çoğu zaman**
	choh-*oo* zah-m*a*hn
I've had it for . . .	**. . . beri var**
	beh-r*ee* vahr
one hour/one day	**Bir saatten/Bir günden**
	beer sah-aht-t*e*hn/beer goohn-d*e*hn
two hours/two days	**İki saatten/İki günden**
	ee-k*ee* sah-aht-t*e*hn/ee-k*ee* goohn-dehn
It's a sharp pain	**Şiddetli bir ağrı**
	shee-deht-l*ee* beer ah-r*u*h
It's a dull pain	**Hafif bir ağrı**
	hah-f*ee*f beer ah-r*u*h
It's a nagging pain	**İçin için sızlıyor**
	ee-ch*ee*n ee-ch*ee*n suhz-l*u*h-yohr
I feel weak	**Kendimi güçsüz hissediyorum**
	kehn-dee-m*ee* goohch-s*oo*hz hees-seh-d*ee*-yoh-room
I feel feverish	**Ateşim var**
	ah-teh-sh*ee*m vahr
I feel dizzy	**Başım dönüyor**
	bah-sh*u*hm der-n*oo*h-yohr
I feel sick	**Midem bulanıyor**
	mee-d*e*hm boo-lah-n*u*h-yohr

Already under treatment for something else?

I take . . . regularly	**Muntazaman . . . alıyorum**
	moon-tah-zah-m*a*hn . . . ah-l*u*h-yoh-room
this medicine	**bu ilâcı**
	boo ee-lah-j*u*h
these pills	**bu hapı**
	boo hah-p*u*h
I have a heart condition	**Kalb hastasıyım**
	kahlb hahs-tah-suh-y*u*hm
I have haemorrhoids	**Hemoroidim var**
	heh-moh-roh-ee-d*ee*m vahr

I have rheumatism	**Romatizmam var**
	roh-mah-teez-m*ah*m vahr
I have diabetes	**Şeker hastasıyım**
	sheh-k*eh*r hahs-tah-suh-y*uh*m
I have asthma	**Astımım var**
	ahs-tuh-m*uh*m vahr
I am pregnant	**Hâmileyim**
	hah-mee-leh-y*eem*
I'm allergic to (pencillin)	**(Penisiline) alerjim var**
	(peh-nee-see-lee-n*eh*) ah-lehr-j*eem* vahr

Other essential expressions

Please can you help?	**Lütfen, yardım edebilir misiniz?**
	l*oo*ht-fehn yahr-d*uh*m eh-deh-bee-l*eer* mee-see-n*eez*
A doctor please	**Doktor, lütfen**
	dohk-t*oh*r l*oo*ht-fehn
A dentist	**Dişçi**
	deesh-ch*ee*
I don't speak Turkish	**Türkçe bilmiyorum**
	T*oo*hrk-cheh b*ee*l-mee-yoh-room
What time does . . . arrive?	**Saat kaçta ∴ . . geliyor?**
	sah-aht kahch-t*ah* . . . gheh-lee-yohr
the doctor	**doktor**
	dohk-toh
the dentist	**dişçi**
	deesh-chee

From the doctor: key sentences to understand

Take this . . .	**. . . bundan alınız**
	boon-d*ah*n ah-luh-n*uz*
every day/every hour	**Her gün/Her saat**
	hehr goohn/hehr sah-*ah*t
(twice/four) times a day	**Günde (iki/dört) defa**
	goohn-d*eh* (ee-k*ee*/derrt) deh-f*ah*
Stay in bed	**Yatakta yatınız**
	yah-tahk-t*ah* yah-tuh-n*uhz*

Don't travel . . .	. . . yolculuk etmeyiniz
	yohl-joo-look eht-meh-yee-neez
for two (days/weeks)	**İki (gün/hafta) için**
	ee-kee (goohn/hahf-tah) ee-cheen
You must go to hospital	**Hastaneye gitmelisiniz**
	hahs-tah-neh-yeh gheet-meh-lee-see-neez

Problems: complaints, loss, theft

ESSENTIAL INFORMATION

- Problems with:
  camping facilities, see p. 32
  household appliances, see p. 48
  health, see p. 86
  the car, see p. 99
- If the worse comes to the worst, find the police station. To ask the way, see p. 17.
- Look for:
  POLİS (Police)
  TURİZM POLİSİ (Tourist Police)
  POLİS KARAKOLU (police station)
- If you lose your passport, go to the nearest British Consulate.
- In an emergency dial 055 for the police and 000 for the fire brigade.

COMPLAINTS

I bought this . . .	. . . bunu aldım
	boo-noo ahl-duhm
today	**Bugün**
	boo-goohn
yesterday	**Dün**
	doohn
on Monday	**Pazartesi günü**
	pah-zahr-teh-see gooh-nooh

[*For days of the week, see p. 122*]

It's no good	**İyi değil**
	ee-yee deh-eel
Look	**Bakınız**
	bah-kuh-nuhz
Here [point]	**Burada**
	boo-rah-dah
Can you change it?	**Bunu değistirebilir misiniz?**
	boo-noo deh-ees-tee-reh-bee-leer mee-see-neez
Here is the receipt	**İşte makbuzu**
	eesh-teh mahk-boo-zoo
Can I have a refund?	**Paramı iade eder misiniz?**
	Pah-rah-muh ee-ah-deh eh-dehr mee-see-neez

LOSS

[See also 'Theft' below: the lists are interchangeable]

I have lost . . .	**. . . kaybettim**
	kay-beht-teem
my bag	**Çantamı**
	chahn-tah-muh
my bracelet	**Bileziğimi**
	bee-leh-zee-ee-mee
my camera	**Fotoğraf makinamı**
	foh-toh-rahf mah-kee-nah-muh
my car keys	**Araba anahtarlarımı**
	ah-rah-bah ah-nah-tahr-lah-ruh-muh
my driving licence	**Şoför ehliyetimi**
	shoh-fer eh-lee-yeh-tee-mee
my insurance certificate	**Sigorta poliçemi**
	see-gohr-tah poh-lee-cheh-mee
my jewellery	**Mücevherlerimi**
	mooh-jehv-hehr-leh-ree-mee
everything!	**Herşeyi**
	hehr-sheh-yee

THEFT

[See also 'Loss' above: the lists are interchangeable]

Someone has stolen . . .	. . . çaldılar
	chahl-duh-lahr
my car	**Arabamı**
	ah-rah-bah-muh
my car radio	**Araba radyomu**
	ah-rah-bah rahd-yoh-moo
my keys	**Anahtarlarımı**
	ah-nah-tahr-lah-ruh-muh
my money	**Paramı**
	pah-rah-muh
my necklace	**Gerdanlığımı**
	ghehr-dahn-luh-uh-muh
my passport	**Pasaportumu**
	pah-sah-pohr-too-moo
my radio	**Radyomu**
	rahd-yoh-moo
my tickets	**Biletlerimi**
	bee-leht-leh-ree-mee
my travellers' cheques	**Seyahat çeklerimi**
	seh-yah-haht chehk-leh-ree-mee
my wallet	**Cüzdanımı**
	joohz-dah-nuh-muh
my watch	**Saatimi**
	sah-aht-tee-mee
my luggage	**Valizlerimi**
	vah-leez-leh-ree-mee

LIKELY REACTIONS: key words to understand

Wait	**Bekleyiniz**
	behk-leh-yee-neez
When?	**Ne zaman?**
	neh zah-mahn
Where?	**Nerede?**
	neh-reh-deh
Name?	**Adı?**
	ah-duh
Address?	**Adresi?**
	ah-dreh-see
I can't help you	**Ben yardım edemiyeceğim**
	behn yahr-duhm eh-deh-mee-yeh-jeh-eem

There's nothing I can do   **Benim yapabileceğim bir şey yok**
beh-n*ee*m yah-pah-bee-leh-jeh-*ee*m
beer shehy yohk

The post office

ESSENTIAL INFORMATION

- To find a post office, see p. 17.
- The sign for post offices in Turkey is PTT
  (black letters on a yellow background).

PTT

- The word for post office is **POSTANE**.
- Main post offices are usually open from 8.00 a.m. until 8.00 p.m.
  In larger towns there is usually a post office open until midnight
  and in the main cities one that stays open twenty-four hours a
  day.
- Stamps are bought at the counter marked **PUL**.
- Post offices also deal with telephoning and telegrams.
- For poste restante you should show your passport at the counter
  marked **POST RESTANT**.

WHAT TO SAY

To England, please   **İngiltere'ye lütfen**
een-gheel-t*e*h-reh-yeh *loo*ht-fehn

[*Hand letters, cards or parcels over the counter*]
To Australia   **Avustralya'ya**
ah-voos-tr*a*hl-yah-yah

To the United States   **Amerika'ya**
ah-meh-ree-k*a*h-yah

[*For other countries, see p. 127*]
How much is . . .   **. . . ne kadar?**
neh kah-d*a*hr

    this parcel (to Canada)?   **Bu koli (Kanada'ya)**
boo koh-l*ee* (kah-n*a*h-dah-yah)

a letter (to Australia)?	**Bir mektub (Avustralya'ya)** beer mehk-*toob* (ah-voos-tr*a*hl- yah-yah)
a postcard to England	**Bir kartpostal (İngiltere'ye)** beer kahrt-pohs-t*a*hl (een-gheel- *teh*-reh-yeh)
Air mail	**Uçak** oo-ch*a*hk
Surface mail	**Normal posta** nohr-mahl p*o*hs-tah
One stamp, please	**Bir pul, lütfen** beer pool l*o*oht-fehn
Two stamps	**İki pul** ee-k*ee* pool
One (one hundred) lira stamp	**Bir (yüz) liralık pul** beer (yoohz) lee-rah-l*u*hk pool
I'd like to send a telegram	**Bir telgraf göndermek istiyorum** beer tehl-gr*a*hf ghern-dehr-m*e*hk ees-*tee*-yoh-room

Telephoning

ESSENTIAL INFORMATION

- In order to make a telephone call from a public callbox you will need a jeton. These are obtainable from post offices (at the counter marked **JETON**) and also from street vendors (cigarette vendors usually sell jetons). Jetons come in three sizes: small, medium and large. Small jetons are used for local calls. Medium and large jetons are useful for long-distance and international calls. Callboxes usually have on them instructions in both Turkish and English. Phone cards are also available. These are called **TELEFON KARTI**.
- There are telephones at post offices; telephone boxes on the streets are yellow or orange.

- If you want to make a long-distance or international call without using jetons, you can do so at the post office. Write the number you want on a piece of paper and hand it over at the counter marked **TELEFON**. You will then be directed to a booth to take the call after it has been dialled for you. Payment for the call is made afterwards at the same counter.
- Most chemists – look for the sign **ECZANE** – have telephones for local calls. You will be given change or sold jetons to put in the slot, or asked to pay after you have made your call. Many local grocery shops have phones as well and operate the same system.
- To make local calls, just dial the number. To make calls outside the city limits or long distance, prefix the number with 9. To make international calls, dial 9, wait for the tone to change, then dial 9 again, followed by the international code and number.
- To call the UK, dial 9-9 44, then the number (minus any initial zero on the area code).
- To call the USA, dial 9-9 1, then the number.
- The telephone system in Turkey has a reputation for being somewhat erratic. It is now much improved; however, you may have to wait for a free line, or dial more than once before you are successful. Above all, be persistent and you will eventually get through!

WHAT TO SAY

Where can I make a telephone call?	**Nereden telefon edebiliyorum?** neh-reh-d*eh*n teh-leh-f*oh*n eh-deh-bee-*lee*-yoh-room
Local/abroad	**Şehir içi/uluslararası** sheh-h*eer* ee-ch*ee*/oo-loos-lahr-ah-rah-s*uh*
I'd like to call this number . . . [*show number*]	**Bu numarayı . . . istiyorum** boo noo-mah-rah-y*uh* . . . ees-*tee*-yoh-room
in England	**İngiltere'de** een-gheel-*t*eh-reh-deh
in Canada	**Kanada'da** kah-n*ah*-dah-dah
in the USA	**Amerika'da** ah-meh-ree-k*ah*-dah

[*For other countries, see p. 127*]

Can you dial it for me, please? **Benim için telefon edebilir misiniz?**
beh-n*ee*m ee-ch*ee*n teh-leh-f*o*hn
eh-deh-bee-l*ee*r mee-see-n*ee*z

How much is it? **Ne kadar?**
neh kah-d*a*hr

Hello! **Alo!**
*a*h-loh

May I speak to . . . **. . . ile konuşmağa olur mu?**
. . . ee-leh koh-noosh-mah-*a*h oh-
l*oo*r moo

Extension . . . **Dahili . . .**
dah-hee-l*ee* . . .

I'm sorry, I don't speak **Özür dilerim, Türkçe bilmiyorum**
Turkish er-z*oo*hr dee-leh-r*ee*m t*oo*hrk-cheh
b*ee*l-mee-yoh-room

Do you speak English? **İngilizce biliyor musunuz?**
Een-ghee-l*ee*z-jeh bee-l*ee*-yohr
moo-soo-n*oo*z

Thank you, I'll phone back **Teşekkür ederim, tekrar ararım**
teh-shehk-k*oo*hr eh-deh-r*ee*m tehk-
r*a*hr ah-rah-r*u*hm

Goodbye **Allahaısmarladık/Hoşça kal**
ahl-lahs-mahr-lah-d*u*hk/hohsh-
ch*a*h kahl

LIKELY REACTIONS

That's (1,500) lira **(Bir bin beş yüz) lira**
(beer been behsh yoohz) l*ee*-rah

Cabin number (3) **Kulübe numarası (üç)**
koo-looh-beh noo-mah-rah-s*u*h
(oohch)

[*For numbers, see p. 118*]

Don't hang up **Ayrılmayınız**
ay-r*u*hl-mah-yuh-nuhz

I'm trying to connect you **Sizi bağlamağa uğraşıyorum**
see-z*ee* bah-lah-mah-*a*h oo-rah-
sh*u*h-yoh-room

You're through **Konuşunuz**
koh-noo-shoo-n*oo*z

There's a delay

Gecikme var
gheh-jeek-meh vahr

I'll try again

Yine deneyeceğim
yee-neh deh-neh-yeh-jeh-eem

Changing cheques and money

ESSENTIAL INFORMATION

- For finding the way to the bank or exchange bureau, see p. 17.
- Look for these words on buildings:
  BANKA
  ... BANKASI] (bank)
  KAMBİYO (change)
- Not all banks will cash Eurocheques. Those that do ask you to make it out in US$ (not Turkish lira or pounds sterling) and then give you TL at the current US$–TL rate.
- You will need your passport when changing money.
- Banks are open 9.00 a.m. – 12.00 noon, 1.30 p.m. – 4.00 p.m.

WHAT TO SAY

I'd like to cash . . .

. . . bozdurmak istiyorum
bohz-door-mahk ees-tee-yoh-room

this travellers' cheque

Bu seyahat çeki
boo seh-yah-haht cheh-kee

these travellers' cheques

Bu seyahat çekleri
boo seh-yah-haht chehk-leh-ree

I'd like to change this into Turkish lira

Bu Türk lirasına için bozdurmak istiyorum
boo toohrk lee-rah-suh-nah ee-cheen bohz-door-mahk ees-tee-yoh-room

Here's . . .

İşte . . .
eesh-teh

my banker's card

banka kartım
bahn-kah kahr-tuhm

my passport	**pasaportum**
	pah-sah-pohr-t*oo*m
What's the rate of exchange?	**Kur ne?**
	koor neh

LIKELY REACTIONS

Passport, please	**Pasaport, lütfen**
	pah-sah-p*o*hrt l*oo*ht-fehn
Sign here	**Burasını imzalayınız**
	boo-rah-suh-n*u*h eem-zah-lah-yuh-n*u*hz
Your banker's card, please	**Banka kartınızı, lütfen**
	b*a*hn-kah kahr-tuh-nuh-z*u*h l*o*oht-fehn
Go to the cash desk	**Vezneye gidiniz**
	vehz-neh-y*e*h ghee-dee-n*ee*z

Car travel

ESSENTIAL INFORMATION

- For finding a filling station or garage, see p. 17.
- Grades of petrol:
  Normal (83–87 octane)
  Süper (90–95 octane)
- For car repairs, look for:
  GARAJ (garage)
  OTOMOBİL TAMİRHANE (car repair workshop)
  OTOMOBİL TAMİRÇİ (car mechanic)
- Petrol stations may be able to help with minor repairs or direct you to a mechanic.
- The equivalent of the AA/RAC in Turkey is the: **Türkiye Turing ve Otomobil Kurumu** (Touring and Automobile Club of Turkey), Halâskârgazi Caddesi 364, Istanbul, Tel: 131 46 31.
- For unfamiliar road signs and warnings, see p. 114.

WHAT TO SAY

[*For numbers, see p. 118*]

(9) litres of . . .	**(Dokuz) litre . . .** (doh-k*oo*z) l*ee*-treh
(2,000) lira of . . .	**(İki bin) lira . . .** (ee-k*ee* b*ee*n) l*ee*-rah
standard/super/diesel	**normal/süper/dizel** nohr-m*ah*l/sooh-p*eh*r/dee-z*eh*l
Fill the tank, please	**Depoyu doldurunuz, lütfen** deh-poh-y*oo* dohl-doo-roo-n*oo*z l*oo*ht-fehn
Will you check . . .	**. . . kontrol eder misiniz?** kohn-tr*oh*l eh-d*eh*r mee-see-n*ee*z
the oil?	**Yağı** yah-*uh*
the battery?	**Aküyü** ah-kooh-y*oo*h
the radiator?	**Radyatörü** rahd-yah-ter-r*oo*h
the tyres?	**Lâstikleri** lahs-teek-leh-r*ee*
I've run out of petrol	**Benzinim bitmiş** behn-zee-n*ee*m beet-m*ee*sh
Can I borrow a can, please?	**Sizden teneke ödünç alabilir miyim?** seez-d*eh*n teh-neh-k*eh* er-d*oo*hnch ah-lah-bee-l*ee*r mee-y*ee*m
My car has broken down	**Arabam bozuldu** ah-rah-b*ah*m boh-zool-d*oo*
My car won't start	**Arabam çalışmıyor** ah-rah-b*ah*m chah-l*uh*sh-muh-yohr
There's been an accident	**Kaza oldu** kah-z*ah* ohl-d*oo*
I've lost my car keys	**Araba anahtarlarımı kaybettim** ah-rah-b*ah* ah-nah-tahr-lah-ruh- m*uh* kay-beht-t*ee*m
My car is . . .	**Arabam . . .** ah-rah-b*ah*m
two kilometres away	**iki kilometre uzakta** ee-k*ee* kee-loh-meh-treh oo-zahk- t*ah*

three kilometres away	**üç kilometre uzakta**
	oohch kee-loh-meh-treh oo-zahk-tah
Can you help me, please?	**Bana yardım edebilir misiniz?**
	bah-nah yahr-duhm eh-deh-bee-leer mee-see-neez
Do you do repairs?	**Tamir yapıyor musunuz?**
	tah-meer yah-puh-yohr moo-soo-nooz
I have a puncture	**Lâstik patladı**
	lahs-teek paht-lah-duh
I have a broken windscreen	**Cam kırıldı**
	jahm kuh-ruhl-duh
I think the problem is here . . . [point]	**Problem şurada galiba**
	proh-blehm shoo-rah-dah gah-lee-bah
I don't know what's wrong	**Nesi var bilmiyorum**
	neh-see vahr beel-mee-yoh-room
Can you repair the fault?	**Tamir edebilir misiniz?**
	tah-meer eh-deh-bee-leer mee-see-neez
Can you come and look?	**Gelip bakabilir misiniz?**
	gheh-leep bah-kah-bee-leer mee-see-neez
Can you estimate the cost?	**Aşağı yukarı ne kadar tutar?**
	ah-shah-uh yoo-kah-ruh neh kah-dahr too-tahr
Can you write it down?	**Yazabilir misiniz?**
	yah-zah-bee-leer mee-see-neez
Do you accept these coupons	**Bu kuponları kabul ediyor musunuz?**
	boo koo-pohn-lah-ruh kah-bool eh-dee-yohr moo-soo-nooz
How long will the repair take?	**Tamir ne kadar sürer?**
	tah-meer neh kah-dahr sooh-rehr
When will the car be ready?	**Araba ne zaman hazır olacak?**
	ah-rah-bah neh zah-mahn hah-zuhr oh-lah-jahk
Can I see the bill?	**Hesaba bakabilir miyim?**
	heh-sah-bah bah-kah-bee-leer mee-yeem
This is my insurance document	**İşte poliçem**
	eesh-teh poh-lee-chehm

1 windscreen wipers	**silecekler** see-leh-jehk-lehr
2 fuses	**sigortalar** see-gohr-tah-lahr
3 heater	**kalorifer** kah-loh-ree-fehr
4 battery	**akü** ah-kooh
5 engine	**motor** moh-tohr
6 fuel pump	**yağ pompası** yah pohm-pah-suh
7 starter motor	**marş** mahrsh
8 carburettor	**karbüratör** kahr-booh-rah-ter
9 lights	**lambalar** lahm-bah-lahr
10 radiator	**radyatör** rahd-yah-ter

11 fan belt	**vantilatör kayışı** vahn-tee-lah-ter kah-yuh-shuh
12 generator	**dinamo** dee-nah-moh
13 brakes	**frenler** frehn-lehr
14 clutch	**debriyaj** deh-bree-yahzh
15 gear box	**şanjman** shahzh-mahn
16 steering	**direksiyon** dee-rehk-see-yohn
17 ignition	**ateşleme** ah-tehsh-leh-meh
18 transmission	**vites** vee-tehs
19 exhaust	**egzoz** ehg-zohz
20 indicator	**sinyal lambaları** seen-yahl lahm-bah-lah-ruh

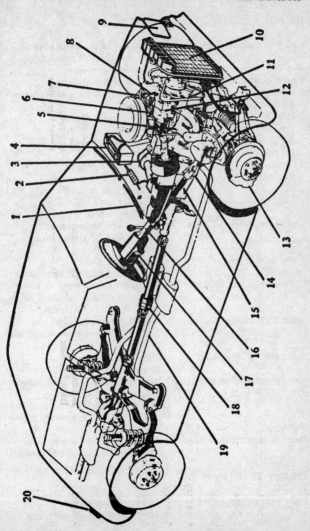

HIRING A CAR

Can I hire a car? **Bir araba kiralıyabilir miyim?**
beer ah-rah-b*a*h kee-rah-luh-yah-
bee-le*er* mee-ye*em*

I need a car . . . **. . . bir araba istiyorum**
beer ah-rah-b*a*h ees-t*ee*-yoh-room

  for two people **İki kişilik**
  ee-ke*e* kee-shee-le*ek*

  for five people **Beş kişilik**
  behsh kee-shee-le*ek*

  for one day **Bir gün için**
  beer goohn ee-ch*ee*n

  for five days **Beş gün için**
  behsh goohn ee-ch*ee*n

  for a week **Bir hafta için**
  beer hahf-t*a*h ee-ch*ee*n

Can you write down . . . **. . . yazabiliyor musunuz?**
yah-zah-bee-le*e*-yohr moo-soo-
n*oo*z

  the deposit to pay? **Depozito ne kadar**
  deh-poh-z*ee*-toh neh kah-d*a*hr

  the charge per kilometre? **Kilometre başına ücret ne kadar**
  kee-loh-m*e*h-treh bah-shuh-n*a*h
  oohch-r*e*ht neh kah-d*a*hr

  the daily charge? **Günlük kirası ne kadar**
  goohn-lo*o*hk kee-rah-s*u*h neh kah-
  d*a*hr

  the cost of insurance? **Sigorta ne kadar**
  see-g*o*hr-tah neh kah-d*a*hr

Can I leave the car in Istanbul? **Arabayı İstanbul'da birakabiliyor
muyum?**
ah-rah-bah-y*u*h ees-t*a*hn-bool-dah
bee-rah-kah-bee-le*e*-yohr moo-
yo*o*m

What documents do I need? **Hangi belgelerim lâzım?**
h*a*hn-ghee behl-gheh-leh-re*e*m l*a*h-
zhum

LIKELY REACTIONS

I don't do repairs **Tamir yapmıyorum**
tah-me*er* yahp-muh-yoh-room

Where's your car	**Arabanız nerede?**
	ah-rah-bah-n*uh*z neh-reh-d*e*h
What make is it?	**Hangi marka?**
	h*a*hn-ghee m*a*hr-kah
Come back (tomorrow/on Monday)	**(Yarın/Pazartesi günü) geliniz**
	(yah-r*uh*n/pah-zahr-teh-s*ee* gooh-noo*h*) gheh-lee-n*ee*z

[For days of the week, see p. 122]

We don't hire cars	**Araba kiralamıyoruz**
	ah-rah-b*a*h kee-rah-l*a*h-muh-yoh-rooz
Your driving licence, please	**Şoför ehliyetiniz, lütfen**
	shoh-f*e*r eh-lee-yeh-tee-n*ee*z l*oo*ht-fehn
The mileage is unlimited	**Sınırsız kilometre**
	suh-nuhr-s*uh*z kee-loh-m*e*h-treh

Public transport

ESSENTIAL INFORMATION

- For finding the way to the bus station, a bus stop, the railway station and a taxi rank, see p. 17.
- Istanbul can be reached by rail from all the major European cities. On the Asian side, one can travel by train, but this method of transport is slow and most people prefer to travel by long-distance buses, which are faster, cheaper and more frequent. The Turkish State Railways are called TCDD (**Türkiye Cumhuriyet Devlet Demiryolları**).
- There is a very extensive network of long-distance buses and minibuses throughout the country. On inter-city buses you can book a seat in advance.
- Municipal buses are red. For these you need to buy tickets in advance to put in the box when you board the bus. Tickets are available at main terminals, and from vendors at all main bus stops. Tickets bought from vendors are very slightly more expensive.

- There are also privately run buses, which are blue. On these you can buy the ticket on board for cash or in exchange for municipal bus tickets.
- **Dolmuş:** a **dolmuş** is a shared car or taxi that travels a fixed route, for which you pay a fixed rate. The cars queue at **dolmuş** ranks, and as soon as a vehicle is full (**dolmuş** means 'full' in Turkish) it sets off. Destinations are marked on signs at the ranks or called out by the drivers. You can get off at any point along the route by asking the driver to stop. Some taxis operate in this way – but check by asking '**Dolmuşmu?**' before you get in.
- Taxis are usually very numerous in the cities and can be picked up at ranks or flagged down on the street. They all have meters, which by law must be in working order. It is wise to make sure that the driver has turned the meter on before setting out. At the end of the journey, pay what is on the meter plus a tip. (Drivers do not always expect tips, but it is becoming the practice to give them and they are much appreciated.)
- One of the great pleasures of Istanbul is travelling on the ferry-boats that link the European and Asian shores of the city and the villages along the shores of the Bosphorus. To get on board, you need to buy a jeton to pass through the turnstiles leading on to the landing stages. Jetons are sold at ticket windows by the turnstiles. If you want to avoid queuing you can also buy jetons from vendors (for a slightly higher price). Express ferries called **Deniz Otobüsleri** (sea buses) run on certain routes.
- Key words on signs (see also p. 114):
  BEKLEME SALONU (waiting room)
  BİLET GİŞESİ (ticket office)
  BÜFE (buffet)
  ÇIKIŞ (exit)
  DANIŞMA BÜROSU (information office)
  DENİZ OTOBÜSÜ (sea bus)
  DOLMUŞ
  EMANET (left luggage office)
  GİRİŞ (entrance)
  İSKELE (ferry landing)
  KAYIP EŞYALAR BÜROSU (lost property office)
  OTOBÜS DURAĞI (bus stop)
  PERON (platform)
  REZERVASYON BÜROSU (booking office)
  SIGARA İÇİLMEZ (no smoking)
  TAKSİ (taxi)

TARİFE (timetable)
TUVALETLER (toilets)
VAPUR (ferryboat)

WHAT TO SAY

Where does the bus (for Ankara) leave from?	**(Ankara'ya) otobüs nereden kalkıyor?** (ahn-kah-rah-yah) oh-toh-boohs neh-reh-dehn kahl-kuh-yohr
At what time does the bus leave (for Ankara)?	**Otobüs (Ankara'ya) saat kaçta kalkıyor?** oh-toh-boohs (ahn-kah-rah-yah) sah-aht kahch-tah kahl-kuh-yohr
At what time does the bus arrive (in Ankara)?	**(Ankara'ya) otobüs saat kaçta varıyor?** (ahn-kah-rah-yah) oh-toh-boohs sah-aht kahch-tah vah-ruh-yohr
Is this the bus (for Ankara)?	**(Ankara'ya) otobüs bu mu?** (ahn-kah-rah-yah) oh-toh-boohs boo moo
Where does the train (for Istanbul) leave from?	**(İstanbul'a) tren nereden kalkıyor?** (ees-tahn-boo-lah) trehn neh-reh-dehn kahl-kuh-yohr
At what time does the train leave (for Istanbul)?	**Tren (İstanbul'a) saat kaçta kalkıyor?** trehn (ees-tahn-boo-lah) sah-aht kahch-tah kahl-kuh-yohr
Is this the train (for Istanbul)?	**(İstanbul) treni bu mu?** (ees-tahn-bool) treh-nee boo moo
Do I have to change?	**Aktarma yapmam lâzım mı?** ahk-tahr-mah yahp-mahn lah-zuhm muh
Where does . . . leave from?	**. . . nereden kalkıyor?** neh-reh-dehn kahl-kuh-yohr
the bus	**Otobüs** oh-toh-boohs
the train	**Tren** trehn
the underground	**Tünel** tooh-nehl

the **dolmuş**	**Dolmuş**
	dohl-m*oo*sh
the ferryboat	**Vapur**
	vah-p*oo*r
for the airport	**hava meydanına**
	hah-v*a*h mehy-dah-nuh-n*a*h
for the mosque	**camiye**
	jah-mee-y*e*h
for the beach	**plaja**
	plah-zh*a*h
for the market	**çarşıya**
	chahr-shuh-y*a*h
for the railway station	**istasyona**
	ees-tahs-yoh-n*a*h
for the town centre	**şehir merkezine**
	sheh-h*ee*r mehr-keh-zee-n*e*h
for the town hall	**belediye dairesine**
	beh-leh-dee-y*e*h dah-ee-reh-see-n*e*h
for the church	**kilise'ye**
	kee-l*ee*-seh-yeh
for the swimming pool	**yüzme havuzuna**
	yoohz-m*e*h hah-voo-zoo-nah
Is this . . .	**. . . bu mu?**
	boo moo
the bus for the market place?	**Çarşıya otobüs**
	chahr-shuh-y*a*h oh-toh-b*oo*hs
the **dolmuş** for the station?	**İstasyona dolmuş**
	ees-tahs-yoh-n*a*h dohl-m*oo*sh
Where can I get a taxi?	**Taksi nerede bulabilirim?**
	tahk-s*ee* neh-reh-d*e*h boo-lah-bee-lee-r*ee*m
Can you put me off at the right stop, please?	**Beni doğru durakta indiriniz, lütfen?**
	beh-n*ee* doh-r*oo* doo-rahk-t*a*h een-dee-ree-n*ee*z l*oo*ht-fehn
Can I book a seat?	**Yer ayırtabiliyor muyum?**
	yehr ah-yuhr-tah-bee-l*ee*-yohr moo-y*oo*m
A single	**Yalnız gidiş**
	yahl-n*u*hz ghee-d*ee*sh

A return	**Gidiş dönüş** ghee-deesh der-noosh
First class	**Birinci mevki** bee-reen-jee mehv-kee
Second class	**İkinci mevki** ee-keen-jee mehv-kee
One adult	**Bir kişi** beer kee-shee
Two adults	**İki kişi** ee-kee kee-shee
and one child	**ve bir çocuk** veh beer choh-jook
and two children	**ve iki çocuk** veh ee-kee choh-jook
How much is it?	**Ne kadar?** neh kah-dahr

LIKELY REACTIONS

Over there	**Orada** oh-rah-dah
Here	**Burada** boo-rah-dah
Platform (1)	**Peron (bir)** peh-rohn (beer)
(At 4) o'clock	**Saat (dörtte)** sah-aht (derrt-teh)
[*For times, see p. 120*] Change (at Ankara)	**(Ankara'da) aktarma yapınız** (ahn-kah-rah-dah) ahk-tahr-mah yah-puh-nuhz
Change (at the market)	**Carşıda aktarma yapınız** chahr-shuh-dah ahk-tahr-mah yah-puh-nuhz
This is your stop	**Durağınız bu** doo-rah-uh-nuhz boo
There's only second class	**Yalnız ikinci mevki var** yahl-nuhz ee-keen-jee mehv-kee vahr
There's a supplement	**Fark ödemiz lâzım** fahrk er-deh-meez lah-zuhm

Leisure

ESSENTIAL INFORMATION

- For finding the way to a place of entertainment, see p. 17.
- For times of day, see p. 120.
- For important signs, see p. 114.

WHAT TO SAY

At what time does . . . open?	**Saat kaçta . . . açılıyor** sah-*ah*t kahch-t*ah* . . . ah-chuh-l*uh*-yohr
the art gallery	**sanat galerisi** sah-n*ah*t gah-leh-ree-s*ee*
the cinema	**sinema** see-neh-m*ah*
the concert hall	**konser salonu** kohn-s*eh*r sah-loh-n*oo*
the disco	**diskotek** dees-koh-t*eh*k
the museum	**müze** mooh-zeh
the night club	**gece kulübü** gheh-jeh koo-looh-b*oo*h
the sports stadium	**stadyum** stahd-y*oo*m
the swimming pool	**yüzme havuzu** yoohz-meh hah-voo-z*oo*
the theatre	**tiyatro** tee-y*ah*-troh
the zoo	**hayvanat bahçesi** hay-vah-n*ah*t bah-cheh-s*ee*
At what time does . . . close?	**Saat kaçta . . . kapanıyor?** sah-aht kahch-t*ah* . . . kah-pah-n*uh*-yohr
the art gallery	**sanat galerisi** sah-n*ah*t gah-leh-ree-s*ee*
[See above list] At what time does . . . start?	**Saat kaçta . . . başlıyor?** sah-*ah*t kahch-t*ah* . . . bahsh-l*uh*-yohr

the cabaret	**kabare** kah-bah-reh
the concert	**konser** kohn-sehr
the film	**filim** fee-leem
the match	**maç** mahch
the play	**piyes** pee-yehs
the wrestling	**güreş** gooh-rehsh
How much is it . . .	**. . . ne kadar?** neh kah-dahr
for an adult?	**Bir kişi** beer kee-shee
for a child?	**Bir çocuk** beer choh-jook
Two adults, please	**İki kişi, lütfen** ee-kee kee-shee looht-fehn
Three children, please	**Üç çocuk, lütfen** oohch choh-jook looht-fehn
Stalls/circle	**Koltuk/balkon** kohl-took/bahl-kohn
Do you have . . .	**. . . var mı?** vahr muh
a programme?	**Program** proh-grahm
a guide book?	**Rehber** reh-behr
Where's the toilet, please?	**Tuvalet nerede, lütfen** too-wah-leht neh-reh-deh looht-fehn
Where's the cloakroom?	**Gardırop nerede?** gahr-duh-rohp neh-reh-deh
I would like lessons in . . .	**. . . dersleri almak istiyorum** dehrs-leh-ree ahl-mahk ees-tee-yoh-room
skiing	**Ski/Kayak** skee/kah-yahk
sailing	**Yelken** yehl-kehn

water skiing	**Su kayağı**
	soo kah-yah-*uh*
sub-aqua diving	**Sualtı sporu**
	soo-ahl-t*uh* spoh-r*oo*
Can I hire . . .	**. . . kiralıyabilir miyim?**
	kee-rah-luh-yah-bee-l*eer* mee-yeem
some skis?	**Kayak**
	kah-y*ah*k
some ski-boots?	**Kayak çizmesi**
	kah-y*ah*k cheez-meh-s*ee*
a boat?	**Bir sandal**
	beer sahn-dahl
a fishing rod?	**Bir olta kamışı**
	beer ohl-t*ah* kah-muh-sh*uh*
a deck chair?	**Bir şezlong**
	beer shehz-l*oh*ng
a sun umbrella?	**Bir güneş şemsiyesi**
	beer gooh-n*eh*sh shehm-see-yeh-see
the necessary equipment?	**Gerekli malzeme**
	gheh-rehk-l*ee* mahl-zeh-m*eh*
How much is it . . .	**. . . ne kadar?**
	neh kah-d*ah*r
per day/per hour?	**Günü/Saati**
	gooh-n*oo*/sah-*ah*-tee
Do I need a licence?	**Ruhsat lâzım mı?**
	roo-hs*ah*t l*ah*-zuhm muh

Asking if things are allowed

ESSENTIAL INFORMATION

Excuse me, please	**Affedersiniz, efendim**
	ahf-feh-dehr-see-n*eez* eh-fehn-deem
Can one . . .	**. . . mi?**
	mee

camp here?	**Burada kamp kurulabilir** boo-rah-dah kahmp koo-roo-lah-bee-leer
come in?	**Buraya girilebilir** boo-rah-yah ghee-ree-leh-bee-leer
dance here?	**Burada dans edilebilir** boo-rah-dah dahns eh-dee-leh-bee-leer
fish here?	**Burada balık tutulabilir** boo-rah-dah bah-luhk too-too-lah-bee-leer
get a drink here?	**Burada içki içilebilir** boo-rah-dah eech-kee ee-chee-leh-bee-leer
get out this way?	**Buradan çıkılabilir** boo-rah-dahn chuh-kuh-lah-bee-leer
get something to eat here?	**Burada bir şey yenilebilir** boo-rah-dah beer shehy yeh-nee-leh-bee-leer
leave one's things here?	**Burada eşya bırakılabilir** boo-rah-dah ehsh-yah bee-rah-kuh-lah-bee-leer
look around here?	**Etrafa bakılabilir** eh-trah-fah bah-kuh-lah-bee-leer
park here?	**Burada park edilebilir** boo-rah-dah pahrk eh-dee-leh-bee-leer
sit here?	**Burada oturulabilir** boo-rah-dah oh-too-roo-lah-bee-leer
smoke here?	**Burada sigara içilebilir** boo-rah-dah see-gah-rah ee-chee-leh-bee-leer
swim here?	**Burada yüzülebilir** boo-rah-dah yooh-zooh-leh-bee-leer
take photos here?	**Burada fotoğraf çekilebilir** boo-rah-dah foh-toh-rahf cheh-kee-leh-bee-leer
telephone here?	**Buradan telefon edilebilir** boo-rah-dahn teh-leh-fohn eh-dee-leh-bee-leer

wait here?	**Burada beklenilebilir** boo-rah-d*ah* behk-leh-nee-leh-bee-*lee*r

LIKELY REACTIONS

Yes, certainly	**Tabii, olur** tah-bee-*ee* oh-l*oo*r
No, certainly not	**Olmaz** ohl-m*ah*z
I think so	**Sanıyorum** sah-n*uh*-yoh-room
Of course	**Tabii** tah-bee-*ee*
Yes, but be careful	**Evet, ama dikkat!** *eh*-veht ah-m*ah* deek-k*ah*t
I don't think so	**Sanmıyorum** s*ah*n-muh-yoh-room
Not normally	**Çoğunlukla, hayır** choh-oon-look-l*ah* h*ah*-yuhr
Sorry	**Özür dilerim** er-z*oo*hr dee-leh-r*ee*m

Reference

PUBLIC NOTICES

- Key words on signs for drivers, pedestrians, travellers, shoppers and overnight guests.

AÇIK	Open
ASANSÖR	Lift
AZAMİ SÜRAT	Speed limit
BAYANLAR	Ladies
BAYLAR	Gentlemen
BENZİN İSTASYONU	Petrol station

BİLETLER	Tickets
BOŞ	Vacant
BOŞ YER YOK	No vacancies
ÇALINIZ	Ring
ÇEKİNİZ	Pull
ÇIKILIR	Way out
ÇIKIŞ	Exit
DANIŞMA	Information
DENİZE GİRİLMEZ	No bathing
DİKKAT	Attention
DİKKAT KÖPEK VAR	Beware of the dog
DOKUNMAYINIZ	Do not touch
DOLU/DOLMUŞTUR	Full
DUR	Stop!
DURAK	Stop (as in bus stop)
DURMAK YASAKTIR	No stopping
EMÂNET	Left luggage
GEÇ	Cross (now)
GEÇİT	Crossing
GEÇMEK YASAKTIR	No overtaking
GERİ DÖNÜLMEZ	No U-turn
GİRİLİR	Way in
GİRİLMEZ	No entry
GİRİNİZ	Enter
GİRİŞ	Entrance
GİRİŞ SERBESTTİR	Entrance free
GİRMEK YASAK(TIR)	Entry forbidden
GİŞE	Ticket office
GÜMRÜK	Customs
HAREKET	Departure
İÇİLMEZ	Not for drinking
İÇME SUYU	Drinking water
İLK YARDIM	First aid
İMDAT ÇIKIŞI	Emergency exit
İSKELE	Landing stage (ferry)
İTİNİZ	Push
İZİNSİZ GİRİLMEZ	No unauthorized entry
JETON GİŞELERİ	Jeton counter
KAMP YAPMAK YASAK	No camping
KAPALI	Closed
KARAKOL	Police station
KAVŞAK	Road junction

KILAVUZ	Guide
KİRALIK	For rent
KUŞET	Couchette
LOKANTA VAGONU	Dining car
MEŞGUL	Occupied
ÖLÜM TEHLİKESİ	Danger of death
OTOBÜS DURAĞI	Bus stop
ÖZEL	Private
PARK YAPILMAZ	No parking
PERONLAR	Platforms
POLİS	Police
SAĞDAN GİDİNİZ	Keep right
SATILIK	For sale
SATIŞLAR	Sales
SICAK	Hot
SİGARA İÇİLMEZ	No smoking
SOĞUK	Cold
SOLDAN GİDİNİZ	Keep left
SON	End
TAŞIT GİREMEZ	No entry for vehicles
TEHLİKE	Danger
TEHLİKELİ MADDE	Dangerous substance
TEK İSTİKAMET	One way
TEK YÖN	One way
TERCÜMAN	Interpreter/translator
TRAFİK POLİSİ	Traffic police
TREN YOLU GEÇİDİ	Level crossing
TUTULMUŞ	Reserved
TUVALET	Toilet
VARIŞ	Arrival
VEZNE	Cashier
VİRAJ	Bend
YASAK(TIR)	Prohibited
YATAKLI VAGON	Sleeping car
YAVAŞ	Slow
YAYA GEÇİDİ	Pedestrian crossing
YOLDA ÇALIŞMA	Road works
YOL KAPALIDIR	Road closed
YOL TAMİRATI	Road repairs

ABBREVIATIONS

AA	Anadolu Ajansı	Anatolia Agency (a press agency)
ABD	Amerika Birleşik Devletleri	USA
Ank.	Ankara	Ankara
apt.	apartman	apartment house
As.	Askeri	Military
As.İz.	Askeri İnzibat	Military Police
ass.	asistan	assistant
AŞ	Anonim Şirketi	Ltd
B.	Bay	Mr
B.	Batı	West
BM	Birleşmiş Milletler	United Nations
BMM	Büyük Millet Meclisi	Grand National Assembly (Turkish parliament)
Bn	Bayan	Mrs, Miss, Ms
Bul.	Bulvar	Boulevard
Cad.	Cadde	Avenue
D.	Doğu	East
DDY	Devlet Deniz Yolları	Turkish State Maritime Lines
Doc.	Doçent	Assistant Professor
Dr	Doktor	Doctor
G.	Güney	South
Gen.	General	General
gr.	gram	gram
İETT	İstanbul Elektrik Tramvay Tünel	Istanbul Municipal Transport
İst.	İstanbul	Istanbul
K.	Kuzey	North
KDV	Katma Değer Vergisi	VAT
kg.	kilogram	kilogram
km.	kilometre	kilometre
Koll.Şti.	Kollektif Şirketi	Ltd
L.	lira	lira
m.	metre	metre
Mah.	Mahalle	district, borough, ward
Mah.	Mahkeme	law court
MÖ	Milâttan önce	BC
MS	Milâttan sonra	AD
No.	numara	number

Ord.Prof.	**Ordinaryüs Profesör**	Professor
Ort.	**Ortaklık**	Private Company
PK	**Posta Kutusu**	post box
PTT	**Posta Telgraf Telefon**	Post, Telegraph and Telephone Office
s.	**sayfa**	page
sm.	**santimetre**	centimetre
Sok.	**Sokak**	Street
TBMM	**Türkiye Büyük Millet Meclisi**	Turkish Grand National Assembly (parliament)
TC	**Türkiye Cumhuriyeti**	Republic of Turkey
TCDD	**Türkiye Cumhuriyeti Devlet Demiryolları**	Turkish State Railways
TDK	**Türk Dil Kurumu**	Turkish Language Society
Tel.	**telefon**	telephone
Telf.	**telefon**	telephone
Telg.	**telgraf**	telegraph
THY	**Türk Hava Yolları**	Turkish Airlines
TM	**Türk Malı**	Made in Turkey
TL	**Türk lirası**	Turkish lira
TRT	**Türkiye Radyo Televizyon Kurumu**	Turkish Radio and Television Corporation
TTOK	**Türkiye Turing ve Otomobil Kurumu**	Touring and Automobile Club of Turkey
v.d.	**ve devamı**	and so on
v.s.	**ve saire**	etc.

NUMBERS

Cardinal numbers

0	**sıfır**	suh-f*uh*r
1	**bir**	beer
2	**iki**	ee-k*ee*
3	**üç**	oohch
4	**dört**	derrt
5	**beş**	behsh
6	**altı**	alh-t*uh*
7	**yedi**	yeh-d*ee*
8	**sekiz**	seh-k*ee*z

9	dokuz	doh-k*ooz*
10	on	ohn
11	on bir	ohn beer
12	on iki	ohn ee-k*ee*
13	on üç	ohn oohch
14	on dört	ohn derrt
15	on beş	ohn behsh
16	on altı	ohn ahl-t*uh*
17	on yedi	ohn yeh-d*ee*
18	on sekiz	ohn seh-k*eez*
19	on dokuz	ohn doh-k*ooz*
20	yirmi	yeer-m*ee*
21	yirmi bir	yeer-m*ee* beer
22	yirmi iki	yeer-m*ee* ee-k*ee*
23	yirmi üç	yeer-m*ee* oohch
24	yirmi dört	yeer-m*ee* derrt
25	yirmi beş	yeer-m*ee* behsh
30	otuz	oh-t*ooz*
35	otuz beş	oh-t*ooz* behsh
40	kırk	kuhrk
45	kırk beş	kuhrk behsh
50	elli	ehl-l*ee*
55	elli beş	ehl-l*ee* behsh
60	altmış	ahlt-m*uh*sh
65	altmış beş	ahlt-m*uh*sh behsh
70	yetmiş	yeht-m*ee*sh
75	yetmiş beş	yeht-m*ee*sh behsh
80	seksen	sehk-sehn
85	seksen beş	sehk-sehn behsh
90	doksan	dohk-s*a*hn
95	doksan beş	dohk-s*a*hn behsh
100	yüz	yoohz
105	yüz beş	yoohz behsh
115	yüz on beş	yoohz ohn behsh
125	yüz yirmi beş	yoohz yeer-m*ee* behsh
200	iki yüz	ee-k*ee* yoohz
205	iki yüz beş	ee-k*ee* yoohz behsh
215	iki yüz on beş	ee-k*ee* yoohz ohn behsh
300	üç yüz	oohch yoohz
400	dört yüz	derrt yoohz
500	beş yüz	behsh yoohz
600	altı yüz	ahl-t*uh* yoohz

700	**yedi yüz**	yeh-d*ee* yoohz
800	**sekiz yüz**	seh-k*eez* yoohz
900	**dokuz yüz**	doh-k*ooz* yoohz
1000	**bin**	been
2000	**iki bin**	ee-k*ee* been
5000	**beş bin**	behsh been
10,000	**on bin**	ohn been
100,000	**yüz bin**	yoohz been
1,000,000	**bir milyon**	beer meel-y*oh*n

Ordinal numbers

1st	**birinci**	bee-reen-j*ee*
2nd	**ikinci**	ee-keen-j*ee*
3rd	**üçüncü**	ooh-choohn-j*ooh*
4th	**dördüncü**	derr-doohn-j*ooh*
5th	**beşinci**	beh-sheen-j*ee*
6th	**altıncı**	ahl-tuhn-j*uh*
7th	**yedinci**	yeh-deen-j*ee*
8th	**sekizinci**	seh-kee-zeen-j*ee*
9th	**dokuzuncu**	doh-koo-zoon-j*oo*
10th	**onuncu**	oh-noon-j*oo*
11th	**on birinci**	ohn bee-reen-j*ee*
12th	**on ikinci**	ohn ee-keen-j*ee*

TIME

What time is it?	**Saat kaç**
	sah-*a*ht kahch
It's . . .	(This is not translated in Turkish)
one o'clock	**Saat bir**
	sah-*a*ht beer
two o'clock	**Saat iki**
	sah-*a*ht ee-k*ee*
three o'clock	**Saat üç**
	sah-*a*ht oohch
four o'clock in the morning	**Sabah saat dört**
	sah-b*a*h sah-*a*ht derrt
in the afternoon	**Öğleden sonra . . .**
	er-leh-d*e*hn s*o*hn-rah
in the evening	**Akşam . . .**
	ahk-sh*a*hm

at night	**Gece . . .** gheh-jeh
It's . . .	(This is not translated in Turkish)
noon	**Öğle** er-leh
half past twelve	**Yarım** yah-ruhm
midnight	**Gece yarısı** gheh-jeh yah-ruh-suh
It's . . .	(This is not translated in Turkish)
five past five	**Beşi beş geçiyor** beh-shee behsh gheh-chee-yohr
ten past five	**Beşi on geçiyor** beh-shee ohn gheh-chee-yohr
a quarter past five	**Beşi çeyrek geçiyor** beh-shee chehy-rehk gheh-chee- yohr
twenty past five	**Beşi yirmi geçiyor** Beh-shee yeer-mee gheh-chee-yohr
twenty-five past five	**Beşi yirmi beş geçiyor** beh-shee yeer-mee behsh gheh- chee-yohr
half past five	**Beş buçuk** behsh boo-chook
twenty-five to six	**Altıya yirmi beş var** ahl-tuh-yah yeer-mee behsh var
twenty to six	**Altıya yirmi var** ahl-tuh-yah yeer-mee vahr
a quarter to six	**Altıya ceyrek var** ahl-tuh-yah chehy-rehk vahr
ten to six	**Altıya on var** ahl-tuh-yah ohn vahr
five to six	**Altıya beş var** ahl-tuh-yah behsh var
At what time . . . (does the bus leave)?	**Saat kaçta . . . (otobüs kalkıyor)?** sah-aht kahch-tah . . . (oh-toh- boohs kahl-kuh-yohr)
At . . .	(In Turkish the 'at' is translated by the suffix **de/da** or **te/ta** added to the end of the number.)
13.00	**On üçte** ohn oohch-teh

14.05	**On dört beşte**
	ohn derrt behsh-*teh*
15.10	**On beş onda**
	ohn behsh ohn-d*ah*
16.15	**On yedi on beşte**
	ohn yeh-d*ee* ohn behsh-*teh*
17.20	**On yedi yirmide**
	ohn yeh-d*ee* yeer-mee-d*eh*
18.25	**On sekiz yirmi beşte**
	ohn seh-k*eez* yeer-m*ee* behsh-*teh*
19.30	**On dokuz otuzda**
	ohn doh-k*ooz* oh-tooz-d*ah*
20.35	**Yirmi otuz beşte**
	yeer-m*ee* oh-t*ooz* behsh-*teh*
21.40	**Yirmi bir kırkta**
	yeer-m*ee* beer kuhrk-t*ah*
22.45	**Yirmi iki kırk beşte**
	yeer-m*ee* ee-k*ee* kuhrk behsh-*teh*
23.50	**Yirmi üç ellide**
	yeer-m*ee* oohch ehl-lee-d*eh*
00.55	**Sıfır elli beşte**
	suh-f*uhr* ehl-l*ee* behsh-*teh*
in ten minutes	**on dakkika sonra**
	ohn dahk-k*ee*-kah s*oh*nn-rah
in a quarter of an hour	**bir çeyrek saat sonra**
	beer chehy-rehk sah-*aht* s*oh*nn-rah
in half an hour	**yarım saat sonra**
	yah-r*uh*m sah-*aht* s*oh*nn-rah
in three-quarters of an hour	**üç çeyrek saat sonra**
	oohch chehy-rehk sah-*aht* s*oh*nn-rah

DAYS

Monday	**Pazartesi**
	pah-z*ah*r-teh-see
Tuesday	**Salı**
	sah-l*uh*
Wednesday	**Çarşamba**
	chahr-sh*ah*m-bah
Thursday	**Perşembe**
	pehr-sh*eh*m-beh
Friday	**Cuma**
	joo-m*ah*

Saturday	**Cumartesi**
	joo-mahr-teh-see
Sunday	**Pazar**
	pah-zahr
last Monday	**geçen pazartesi**
	gheh-chehn pah-zahr-teh-see
next Tuesday	**gelecek salı**
	gheh-leh-jehk sah-luh
on Wednesday	**Çarsamba günü**
	chahr-shahm-bah gooh-nooh
on Thursdays	**Perşembe günleri**
	pehr-shehm-beh goohn-leh-ree
until Friday	**Cumaya kadar**
	joo-mah-yah kah-dahr
until Saturday	**Cumartesiye kadar**
	joo-mahr-teh-see-yeh kah-dahr
before Sunday	**Pazardan önce**
	pah-zahr-dahn ern-jeh
before Monday	**Pazartesiden önce**
	pah-zahr-teh-see-dehn ern-jeh
after Wednesday	**Çarşambadan sonra**
	chahr-shahm-bah-dahn sohn-rah
after Thursday	**Perşembeden sonra**
	pehr-shehm-beh-dehn sohn-rah
the day before yesterday	**evvelki gün**
	ehv-vehl-kee goohn
two days ago	**iki gün önce**
	ee-kee goohn ern-jeh
yesterday	**dün**
	doohn
yesterday morning	**dün sabah**
	doohn sah-bah
yesterday afternoon	**dün öğleden sonra**
	doohn er-leh-dehn sohn-rah
last night	**dün gece**
	doohn gheh-jeh
today	**bugün**
	boo-goohn
this morning	**bu sabah**
	boo sah-bah
this afternoon	**bu öğleden sonra**
	boo er-leh-dehn sohn-rah

tonight	**bu gece**
	boo gheh-jeh
tomorrow	**yarın**
	yah-ruhn
tomorrow morning	**yarın sabah**
	yah-ruhn sah-bah
tomorrow afternoon	**yarın öğleden sonra**
	yah-ruhn er-leh-dehn sohn-rah
tomorrow evening	**yarın akşam**
	yah-ruhn ahk-shahm
tomorrow night	**yarın gece**
	yah-ruhn gheh-jeh
the day after tomorrow	**öbür gün**
	er-boohr goohn

MONTHS AND DATES

January	**Ocak**
	oh-jahk
February	**Şubat**
	shoo-baht
March	**Mart**
	mahrt
April	**Nisan**
	nee-sahn
May	**Mayıs**
	mah-yuhs
June	**Haziran**
	hah-zee-rahn
July	**Temmuz**
	tehm-muhz
August	**Ağustos**
	ah-oos-tohs
September	**Eylül**
	ehy-loohl
October	**Ekim**
	eh-keem
November	**Kasım**
	kah-suhm
December	**Aralık**
	ah-rah-luhk

in January	**ocakta**
	oh-jahk-t*a*h
in June	**haziranda**
	hah-zee-rahn-d*a*h
in September	**eylülde**
	ey-loohl-d*e*h
until February	**şubata kadar**
	shoo-baht-t*a*h kah-d*a*hr
until July	**temmuze kadar**
	tehm-moo-z*e*h kah-d*a*hr
before March	**marttan önce**
	mahrt-t*a*hn ern-j*e*h
before April	**nisandan önce**
	nee-sahn-d*a*hn ern-j*e*h
after May	**mayıstan sonra**
	mah-yuhs-t*a*hn s*o*hn-rah
during June	**haziran içinde**
	hah-zee-r*a*hn ee-cheen-d*e*h
not before July	**temmuzdan önce değil**
	teh-m*o*oz-d*a*hn ern-j*e*h deh-*ee*l
the beginning of August	**ağustosun başı**
	ah-oos-toh-s*oo*n bah-sh*u*h
the middle of September	**eylülün ortası**
	ey-looh-l*oo*hn ohr-tah-s*u*h
the end of October	**ekimin sonu**
	eh-kee-m*ee*n soh-n*oo*
last month	**geçen ay**
	gheh-ch*e*hn ay
this month	**bu ay**
	boo ay
next month	**gelecek ay**
	gheh-leh-j*e*hk ay
in spring	**ilkbaharda**
	eelk-bah-hahr-d*a*h
in summer	**yazda**
	yahz-d*a*h
in autumn	**sonbaharda**
	sohn-bah-hahr-d*a*h
in winter	**kışta**
	kuhsh-t*a*h
this year	**bu yıl**
	boo yuhl

last year	**geçen yıl**
	gheh-chehn yuhl
next year	**gelecek yıl**
	gheh-leh-jehk yuhl
in 1985	**bin dokuz yüz seksen beşte**
	been doh-kooz yoohz sehk-sehn behsh-teh
in 1992	**bin dokuz yüz doksan ikide**
	been doh-kooz yoohz dohk-sahn ee-kee-deh
What's the date today?	**Bugün tarihi ne**
	boo-goohn tah-ree-hee neh
It's 6th March	**Altı mart**
	ahl-tuh mahrt
12th April	**On iki nisan**
	ohn ee-kee nee-sahn
21st August	**Yirmi bir ağustos**
	yeer-mee beer ah-oos-tohs

Public holidays

1 January	**Yılbaşı**	New Year's Day
23 April	**23 Nisan Çocuk Bayramı**	National Sovereignty and Children's Day
19 May	**Gençlik ve Spor Bayramı**	Youth and Sport Day
30 August	**Zafer Bayramı**	Victory Day
28–9 October	**Cumhuriyet Bayramı**	Republic Days

Religious festivals

- The two most important festivals in the Islamic calendar in Turkey are the **Şeker Bayramı** (Sugar Festival), when Muslims celebrate the end of **Ramadan** – the month of fasting – with three and a half days of holiday and feasting; and, three months later, the **Kurban Bayramı** (Feast of the Sacrifice), which lasts for four and a half days. Since the times of the festivals are calculated according to the lunar calendar they fall on different days every year, gradually moving through all the months of the year.
- The Christians and Jews of Turkey also, of course, celebrate their own holy days at the appropriate times.

COUNTRIES AND NATIONALITIES

Countries

Australia	**Avustralya** ah-voos-tr*a*hl-yah
Austria	**Avusturya** ah-*voo*s-toor-yah
Belgium	**Belçika** behl-chee-k*a*h
Britain	**Britanya** bree-t*a*hn-yah
Canada	**Kanada** kah-n*a*h-dah
Czechoslovakia	**Çekoslovakya** cheh-koh-sloh-vahk-y*a*h
East Africa	**Doğu Afrika** doh-*oo* ahf-ree-k*a*h
East Germany	**Doğu Almanya** doh-*oo* ahl-m*a*hn-yah
Eire	**İrlanda** eer-l*a*hn-dah
England	**İngiltere** een-gheel-t*e*h-reh
France	**Fransa** fr*a*hn-sah
Greece	**Yunanistan** yoo-nah-nee-st*a*hn
India	**Hindistan** heen-dee-st*a*hn
Italy	**İtalya** ee-t*a*hl-yah
Luxembourg	**Luksemburg** loohk-sehm-b*oo*rg
Netherlands	**Holanda** hoh-l*a*hn-dah
New Zealand	**Yeni Zelanda** yeh-n*ee* zeh-l*a*hn-dah
Northern Ireland	**Kuzey İrlanda** koo-z*e*hy eer-l*a*hn-dah
Pakistan	**Pakistan** p*a*h-kee-stahn

Poland	**Polonya**
	poh-lohn-yah
Portugal	**Portekiz**
	pohr-teh-keez
Scotland	**İskoçya**
	ees-kohch-yah
South Africa	**Güney Afrika**
	gooh-nehy ahf-ree-kah
Spain	**Ispanya**
	ees-pahn-yah
Switzerland	**İsviçre**
	ees-veech-reh
Turkey	**Türkiye**
	toohr-kee-yeh
USSR	**Sovyetler**
	sohv-yeht-lehr
Wales	**Galler**
	gahl-lehr
West Germany	**Batı Almanya**
	bah-tuh ahl-mahn-yah
West Indies	**Antiller**
	ahn-teel-lehr
Yugoslavia	**Yugoslavya**
	yoo-goh-slahv-yah

Nationalities

American	**Amerikalı**
	ah-meh-ree-kah-luh
Australian	**Avustralyalı**
	ah-voos-trahl-yah-luh
British	**Britanyalı**
	bree-tahn-yah-luh
Canadian	**Kanadalı**
	kah-nah-dah-luh
East African	**Doğu Afrikalı**
	doh-oo ahf-ree-kah-luh
English	**İngiliz**
	een-ghee-leez
Greek	**Yunanlı**
	yoo-nahn-luh

Indian	**Hintli**
	heent-l*ee*
Irish	**İrlandalı**
	eer-l*a*hn-dah-luh
New Zealander	**Yeni Zelandalı**
	yeh-n*ee* zeh-l*a*hn-dah-luh
Pakistani	**Pakistanlı**
	p*a*h-kee-stahn-luh
Scots	**İskoçyalı**
	ees-k*o*hch-yah-luh
South African	**Guney Afrikalı**
	gooh-n*e*hy ahf-ree-kah-l*u*h
Welsh	**Galler**
	gahl-l*e*hr
West Indian	**Antilli**
	ahn-teel-l*ee*
Yugoslav	**Yugoslav**
	yoo-goh-sl*a*hv

DEPARTMENT STORE AND SHOP GUIDE

- Department stores are only just beginning to appear in Turkey,
  so one still has to go to a variety of shops to buy different items.
  This list has been compiled to help with shopping in general.

Antikacı	Antique dealer
Ayakkabıcı	Shoemaker
Ayakkabı tamircisi	Shoe repairer
Bakırcı	Coppersmith
Bakkal	Greengrocer
Balıkçı	Fishmonger
Battaniyeler	Blankets
Berber	Barber
Çantalar	Bags
Çarşaflar	Sheets
Çiçekçi	Florist
Çorap	Socks
Derici	Leather shop
Eczane	Chemist
Elbise	Clothes
Eldivenci	Gloves
Erkek kuaför	Barber

Eşarp	Scarves (for women)
Etekler	Skirts
Fotografçı	Photography shop
Fotokopi	Photocopying
Gazeteci	Newsagent
Gömlekçi	Shirtmaker
Güzellik salonu	Beauty salon
Halıcı	Carpet seller
Hatıra eşyası	Souvenirs
Havlular	Towels
Hırdavatçı	Ironmonger
Kadın çamaşırı	Lingerie
Kadın çorabı	Stockings
Kadın şapkacısı	Milliner
Kadın terzisi	Dressmaker
Kapalı çarşı	Bazaar ('covered market')
Kaşkol	Scarves (for men)
Kazaklar	Pullovers
Kemerler	Belts
Kırtasiyeci	Stationer
Kitabevi	Bookshop
Kuaför	Hairdresser
Kumaşçı	Draper
Kunduracı	Shoemaker
Kuru temizleyici	Dry cleaner
Kuyumcu	Goldsmith
Külotlu çorap	Tights
Kürkçü	Furrier
Lüleci	Pipe-maker
Manav	Greengrocer
Mandıra	Dairy
Mantolar	Women's coats
Mayolar	Bathing suits
Mobilya	Furniture
Mobilyacı	Furniture shop
Mücevherci	Jeweller
Nalbur	Hardware
Oyuncakçı	Toy shop
Paltolar	Overcoats
Pantalonlar	Trousers
Parfümöri	Parfumerie
Pastacı	Confectioner

Pastane	Cake shop
Saatçi	Watchmaker
Sarraf	Moneychanger
Seramik	Ceramics, chinaware
Seyahat acentası	Travel agent
Spor mağazası	Sports shop
Sütçü	Milkman
Şapkacı	Hatter
Şarapçı	Wine merchant
Şarap tüccarı	Wine merchant
Şarkütöri	Delicatessen
Şekerci	Confectioner
Şekerleme	Confectionery
Şemsiyeler	Umbrellas
Tatlıcı	Pastry shop
Terlik	Slippers
Terzi	Tailor
Turizm acentası	Travel agent
Tuhafiyeci	Haberdashery
Tütüncü	Tobacconist
Zücaciyeci	Glassware

CONVERSION TABLES

Read the centre column of these tables from right to left to convert from metric to imperial and from left to right to convert from imperial to metric e.g. 5 litres = 8.80 pints; 5 pints = 2.84 litres

pints		litres		gallons		litres
1.76	1	0.57		0.22	1	4.55
3.52	2	1.14		0.44	2	9.09
5.28	3	1.70		0.66	3	13.64
7.07	4	2.27		0.88	4	18.18
8.80	5	2.84		1.00	5	22.73
10.56	6	3.41		1.32	6	27.28
12.32	7	3.98		1.54	7	31.82
14.08	8	4.55		1.76	8	36.37
15.84	9	5.11		1.98	9	40.91

ounces		grams
0.04	1	28.35
0.07	2	56.70
0.11	3	85.05
0.14	4	113.40
0.18	5	141.75
0.21	6	170.10
0.25	7	198.45
0.28	8	226.80
0.32	9	255.15

pounds		kilos
2.20	1	0.45
4.41	2	0.91
6.61	3	1.36
8.82	4	1.81
11.02	5	2.27
13.23	6	2.72
15.43	7	3.18
17.64	8	3.63
19.84	9	4.08

inches		centimetres
0.39	1	2.54
0.79	2	5.08
1.18	3	7.62
1.58	4	10.16
1.95	5	12.70
2.36	6	15.24
2.76	7	17.78
3.15	8	20.32
3.54	9	22.86

yards		metres
1.09	1	0.91
2.19	2	1.83
3.28	3	2.74
4.37	4	3.66
5.47	5	4.57
6.56	6	5.49
7.66	7	6.40
8.65	8	7.32
9.84	9	8.23

miles		kilometres
0.62	1	1.61
1.24	2	3.22
1.86	3	4.83
2.49	4	6.44
3.11	5	8.05
3.73	6	9.66
4.35	7	11.27
4.97	8	12.87
5.59	9	14.48

A quick way to convert kilometres to miles: divide by 8 and multiply by 5. To convert miles to kilometres: divide by 5 and multiply by 8.

fahrenheit (°F)	centigrade (°C)		lbs/ sq in	k/ sq cm
212°	100° boiling point		18	1.3
100°	38°		20	1.4
98.4°	36.9° body temperature		22	1.5
86°	30°		25	1.7
77°	25°		29	2.0
68°	20°		32	2.3
59°	15°		35	2.5
50°	10°		36	2.5
41°	5°		39	2.7
32°	0° freezing point		40	2.8
14°	−10°		43	3.0
−4°	−20°		45	3.2
			46	3.2
			50	3.5
			60	4.2

To convert °C to °F: divide by 5, multiply by 9 and add 32. To convert °F to °C: take away 32, divide by 9 and multiply by 5.

CLOTHING SIZES

Remember – always try on clothes before buying. Clothing sizes are usually unreliable.

women's dresses and suits

Europe	38	40	42	44	46	48
UK	32	34	36	38	40	42
USA	10	12	14	16	18	20

men's suits and coats

Europe	46	48	50	52	54	56
UK and USA	36	38	40	42	44	46

men's shirts

Europe	36	37		38	39		41	42		43
UK and USA	14	14½		15	15½		16	16½		17

socks

Europe	38–39	39–40	40–41	41–42	42–43
UK and USA	9½	10	10½	11	11½

shoes

Europe	34	35½	36½	38	39	41	42	43	44	45
UK	2	3	4	5	6	7	8	9	10	11
USA	3½	4½	5½	6½	7½	8½	9½	10½	11½	12½

Do it yourself

Some notes on the language

This section does not deal with 'grammar' as such. The purpose here is to explain some of the most obvious and elementary nuts and bolts of the language, based on the principal phrases included in the book. This information should enable you to produce numerous sentences of your own making.

There is no pronunciation in this section, partly because it would get in the way of the explanations and partly because you have to do it yourself at this stage if you are serious – work out the pronunciation from all the earlier examples in the book.

NOUNS

- **Singular:** the word for a/an in Turkish is **bir** ('one'). However, when referring to a noun in general, the noun is used without an article of any kind. Similarly, the noun on its own can also mean some/any.
- **Plural:** the plural is formed by adding **-ler/-lar** to the end of the noun.

	Singular		Plural
an address	adres	addresses	adresler
an apple	elma	apples	elmalar
a beer	bira	beers	biralar
a bill	hesap	bills	hesaplar
a bus	otobüs	buses	otobüsler
a (cup of) tea	çay	teas	çaylar
a key	anahtar	keys	anahtarlar
a menu	mönü	menus	mönüler
a newspaper	gazete	newspapers	gazeteler
a receipt	makbuz	receipts	makbuzlar
a restaurant	lokanta	restaurants	lokantalar
a roll	sandviç	rolls	sandviçler
a room	oda	rooms	odalar
a telephone	telefon	telephones	telefonlar
a timetable	tarife	timetables	tarifeler

- When adding **-ler/-lar** to make the noun plural, how do you choose which ending to use? This depends on the last vowel of the noun. If it is:

  e, i, ö, ü   add   **ler**

  a, ı, o, u   **lar**

  This is called the principle of vowel harmony, whereby the vowels of endings added to words (for instance, to form plurals) change to harmonize with the sound of the root word.

- Does it matter? Not unless you want to make a serious attempt to speak correctly and scratch below the surface of the language. You would generally be understood whichever of the plural endings you added to a noun. However, if you listen to what people say, you will soon pick up which is the correct one to add.

Using the words in the above table, practise saying and writing these sentences in Turkish:

Have you got a receipt?	**Makbuz var mı?**
a telephone?	**. . . var mı?**
I'd like a beer	**Bira istiyorum**
some rolls	**. . . istiyorum**
Where can I get a newspaper?	**Gazete nerede bulabilirim?**
a cup of tea?	**. . . nerede bulabilirim?**
Is there a key?	**Anahtar var mı?**
a telephone?	**. . . var mı?**
a timetable?	
a restaurant?	
a menu?	
Are there any rooms?	**Odalar var mı?**
any newspapers?	**. . . var mı?**
any keys?	

Now try to make up more sentences along these same lines using other vocabulary in the book.

THE

- There is no word for 'the' in Turkish. But if a word is the object of a sentence a vowel ending is added to the word. Once again this vowel is chosen according to the principle of vowel harmony.

- If the final vowel of the noun is: **e** or **i** add **i**

ö ü	**ü**
a ı	**ı**
o u	**u**

- If the noun actually ends in a vowel, a **-y** is inserted as a buffer between the root word and the vowel ending.

address	**adresi**	addresses	**adresleri**
apple	**emlayı**	apples	**elmaları**
beer	**birayı**	beers	**biraları**
bill	**hesabı**	bills	**hesapları**
bus	**otobüsü**	buses	**otobüsleri**
cup of tea	**çayı**	cups of tea	**çayları**
key	**anahtarı**	keys	**anahtarları**
menu	**mönüyü**	menus	**mönüleri**
newspaper	**gazeteyi**	newspapers	**gazeteleri**
receipt	**makbuzu**	receipts	**makbuzları**
restaurant	**lokantayı**	restaurants	**lokantaları**
roll	**sandviçi**	rolls	**sandviçleri**
room	**odayı**	rooms	**odaları**
telephone	**telefonu**	telephones	**telefonları**
timetable	**tarifeyi**	timetables	**tarifeleri**

Using the words in the table above, practise saying and writing these sentences in Turkish:

Have you got the key?	**Anahtarı var mı?**
the timetable?	**. . . var mı?**
the address?	
the menu?	
I'd like the receipt	**Makbuzu istiyorum**
the bill	**. . . istiyorum**
the keys	
Where is the timetable?	**Tarifeyi nerede?**
the key?	**. . . nerede?**
the address?	
the restaurant?	
the room?	

Where are the rolls?	**Sandviçleri nerede?**
the keys?	**. . . nerede?**
the apples?	
the rooms?	
the buses?	
Where can I get the address?	**Adresi nerede bulabilirim?**
the key?	**. . . nerede bululabilirim?**
the	
timetables?	

VAR/YOK

- There is no word, in the English sense, for 'have' in Turkish. Instead, the words **var** (literally, 'existent') and **yok** (literally, 'non-existent') are used. To make these words into questions, **var** is followed by the word **mı**, and **yok** by the word **mu**:

Is there/are there?	**Var mı?**
Isn't there/aren't there?	**Yok mu?**

- In reply, you will hear:

Var	There is/there are
Yok	There isn't/there aren't (any)

Practise writing and saying these sentences in Turkish (remembering that to say 'some/any', just use the word on its own):

Have you got some coffee?	**Kahve var mı?**
some wine?	**. . . var mı?**
some bread?	
Is there any water?	**Su var mı?**
any cheese?	**. . . var mı?**
any tea?	
Are there any keys?	
Isn't there any beer?	**Bira yok mu?**
any water?	**. . . yok mu?**
any wine?	
Aren't there any newspapers?	

THIS/THAT

Use these three words in Turkish:

Bu this	**Şu** that (nearby)	**O** that (further away)

If you don't know the Turkish for something you can use these words, pointing to what you want. If you use them with a verb, add **-nu** to the end of them:

Bunu istiyorum	I want this
Şunu istiyorum	I want that
Onu istiyorum	I want that (over there)
Bunu istiyorum	I need this

HELPING OTHERS

You can help yourself with phrases such as:

I'd like . . . a roll	**Sandviç . . . istiyorum**
Where can I get . . . a (cup of) tea?	**Çay . . . nerede bulabilirim?**
I need . . . a receipt	**Makbuz . . . istiyorum**
I'd like . . . a beer	**Bira . . . istiyorum**

If you come across a compatriot having trouble making himself or herself understood, you should be able to speak to the Turkish person on their behalf. (A pronunciation guide is provided from here on, to help you with the unfamiliar parts of each phrase.)

● Note that you use the same verb form for he or she in Turkish.

He'd like . . .	**Sandviç . . . istiyor**
	sahnd-v*ee*ch . . . ees-*tee*-yohr
She'd like . . .	**Bira . . . istiyor**
	bee-rah . . . ees-*tee*-yohr
Where can he get . . .?	**Çay . . . nerede bulabilir?**
	chay . . . neh-reh-d*e*h boo-lah-bee-leer
Where can she get . . .?	**Sandviç . . . nerede bulabilir?**
	sahnd-v*ee*ch . . . neh-reh-d*e*h boo-lah-bee-leer
He'll have . . .	**Çay . . . ister**
	chay . . . ees-t*e*hr
She'll have . . .	**Neskafe . . . ister**
	nehs-kah-f*e*h . . . ees-t*e*hr
He needs . . .	**Makbuz . . . istiyor**
	mahk-b*ooz* . . . ees-*tee*-yohr
She needs . . .	**Bilet . . . istiyor**
	bee-l*e*ht ees-*tee*-yohr

You can also help a couple or a group if they are having difficulties.

- To make the plural 'they' form of the verb, add **-ler/-lar** to the he/she form, following the same rule of vowel harmony described above in the section on forming plural nouns.

They'd like . . .	**Peynir . . . istiyorlar**
	pehy-n*ee*r . . . ees-tee-yohr-l*a*hr
Where can they get . . .?	**Aspirin . . . nerede bulabilirler?**
	ahs-pee-r*ee*n . . . neh-reh-d*e*h boo-lah-bee-leer-l*e*hr
They'll have . . .	**Şarap . . . isterler**
	shah-r*a*hp . . . ees-tehr-l*e*hr
They need . . .	**Şu . . . istiyorlar**
	shoo . . . ees-tee-yohr-l*a*r

What about the two of you? No problem. Once again you change the verb ending.

- Taking the he/she form of the verb, if the final vowel is:

e or i	add	**iz**
ö	ü	**üz**
a	ı	**ız**
o	u	**uz**

We'd like . . .	**Şarap . . . istiyoruz**
	shah-r*a*hp . . . ees-t*ee*-yoh-rooz
Where can we get . . .?	**Şu . . . nerede bulabiliriz?**
	shoo . . . neh-reh-d*e*h boo-lah-bee-l*ee*-reez
We'll have . . .	**Bira . . . isteriz**
	b*ee*-rah . . . ees-t*e*h-reez
We need . . .	**Aspirin . . . istiyoruz**
	ahs-pee-r*ee*n . . . ees-t*ee*-yoh-rooz

USEFUL WORDS

Try writing out and memorizing these six useful words:

I want/need	**İstiyorum**
	ees-t*ee*-yoh-room

I don't want/need	**İstemiyorum** ees-teh-mee-yoh-room
I know	**Biliyorum** bee-lee-yoh-room
I don't know	**Bilmiyorum** beel-mee-yoh-room
I understand	**Anlıyorum** ahn-luh-yoh-room
I don't understand	**Anlamıyorum** ahn-lah-muh-yoh-room

MORE PRACTICE

Here are some more Turkish names of things. See how many different sentences you can make up, using the various points of information given earlier in this section.

		Singular	Plural
1	ashtray	**küllük**	**küllükler**
2	bag	**çanta**	**çantalar**
3	car	**araba**	**arabalar**
4	cigarette	**sigara**	**sigaralar**
5	corkscrew	**tirbuşon**	**tirbuşonlar**
6	deckchair	**şezlong**	**şezlonglar**
7	garage (repairs)	**tamirhane**	**tamirhaneler**
8	grapes	**üzüm**	**üzümler**
9	ice-cream	**dondurma**	**dondurmalar**
10	melon	**kavun**	**kavunlar**
11	passport	**pasaport**	**pasaportlar**
12	postcard	**kartpostal**	**kartpostallar**
13	salad	**salata**	**salatalar**
14	shoe	**ayakkabı**	**ayakkabılar**
15	stamp	**pul**	**pullar**
16	station	**istasyon**	**istasyonlar**
17	suitcase	**valiz**	**valizler**
18	telephone	**telefon**	**telefonlar**
19	telephone jeton	**jeton**	**jetonlar**
20	ticket	**bilet**	**biletler**

Index